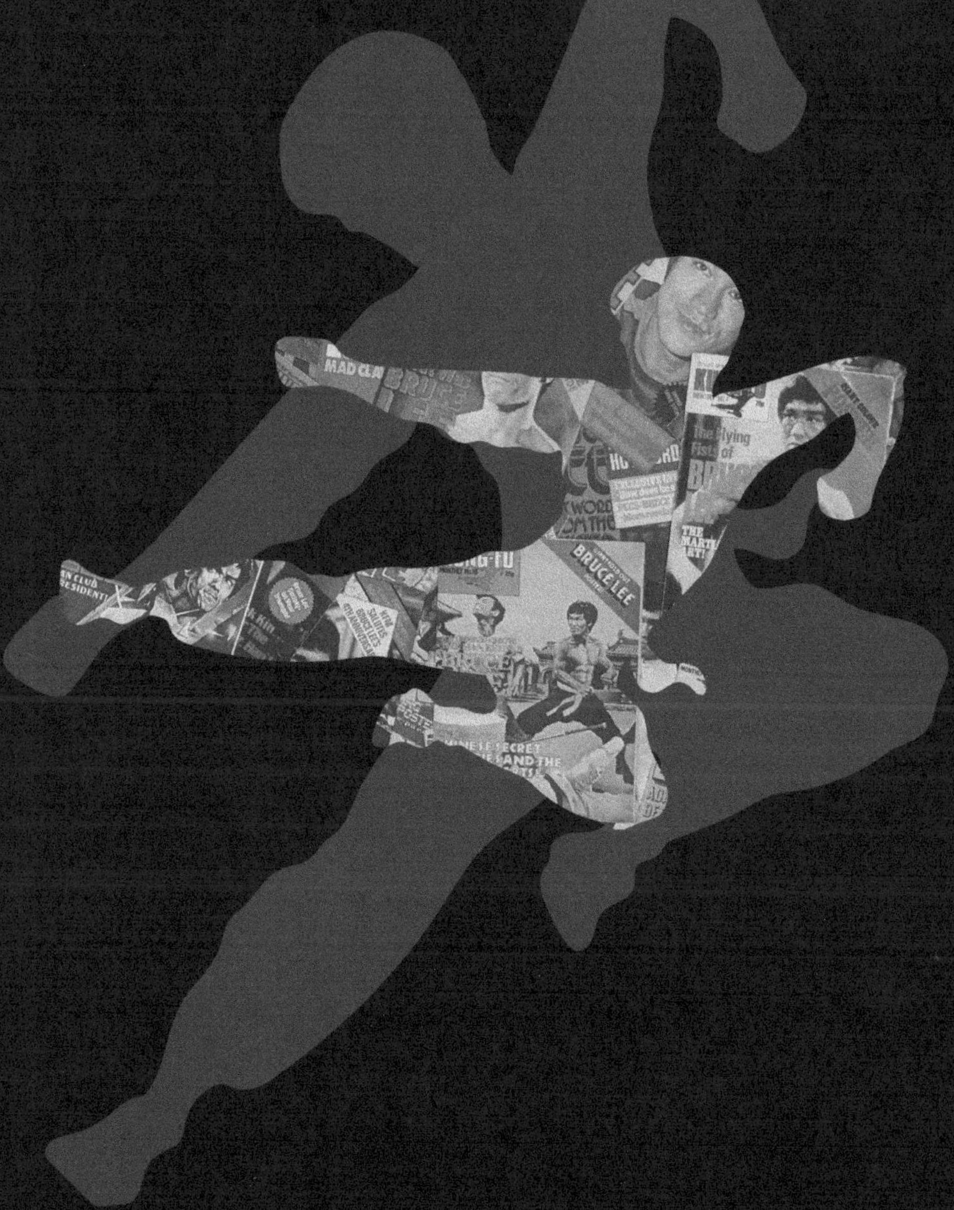

KUNG-FU
MONTHLY

THE ARCHIVE SERIES

THE WISDOM OF BRUCE LEE

WRITTEN BY
ROGER HUTCHINSON & FELIX DENNIS

COMPILED AND EDITED BY
CARL FOX & ANDREW STATON

PIT WHEEL PRESS
BARNSLEY

Published by
PIT WHEEL PRESS LIMITED
www.pitwheelpress.com

Copyright © 2022 Pit Wheel Press Limited. All Right Reserved. No part of this book may be reproduced, scanned or distributed in any printed or electronic form without permission.

THE WISDOM OF BRUCE LEE

Copyright © 1976 by H. Bunch Associates Ltd. (except where copyright on certain photographic material already exists). This publication or any parts thereof may not be reproduced in any form whatsoever without permission in writing from the copyright proprietor.

A Pit Wheel Press edition, published by special arrangement with Dennis Publishing, London.

First Printing 1976
Revised Edition 2022

Printed in the United Kingdom
ISBN 978-1-915414-06-9

BRUCE LEE is a trademark of Bruce Lee Enterprises, LLC.

IN MEMORY OF
SIFU DAVE CARNELL
*The Ultimate British Jeet Kune Do Master
He Would Have Loved This Book*

ACKNOWLEDGEMENTS

I would like to thank the following people for their help and participation in the making of this book:

James Bishop
Andrew Kimura
John Little
John Overall
Carlotta Serantoni
Tim Tackett

Special Thanks
Roger Hutchinson

CREDITS

Original 1976 Edition

Don Atyeo, Paul Simmons, Jonathon Green, Peter Bennett
Cathay Films (UK), Golden Harvest Films (Hong Kong)
Warner Bros Films (UK), Concord Films (Hong Kong)
Chang Vung Djih, Paul Chang & Rex Features Ltd.
Black & White Photographs by **Chester Maydole.**
Design by **Perry Neville.** *Filmsetting by* **Letterbox Ltd.**

The Kung-Fu Monthly Archive Series

Research, Editing, Layout & Design
Carl Fox

Research
Andrew Staton

Photograph Acknowlegements
Kung-Fu Monthly, Roger Hutchinson & Carl Fox

Kung-Fu Monthly Collage Image
Copyright © 2022 Carl Fox

BRUCE LEE
IN HIS OWN WORDS

Bruce Lee was a man of action. Rarely in one human being has such speed, strength, and skill been developed to such a high degree of excellence. But he was also a man of great depth and sensitivity. Between the sweet and the pain, the work and the fame, he always found a way to express some profound ideas in but a few words.

"Man, because he is a creative individual,
is far more important than any style or system."

"Life is a constant process of relating."

"Knowing is not enough; we must apply.
Willing is not enough; we must do."

"A goal is not always meant to be reached,
it often serves simply as something to aim at."

"Optimism is a faith that leads to success."

"Knowledge will give you power,
but character will give you respect."

"If you think a thing is impossible,
you'll make it impossible."

"If you love life, don't waste time,
for time is what life is made up of."

"Life is an ever-flowing process and somewhere
on the path some unpleasant things will pop up - it
might leave a scar, but then life is flowing on, and
like running water, when it stops, it grows stale.
Go bravely on because each experience
teaches us a lesson."

KUNG-FU MONTHLY

THE ARCHIVE SERIES
THE WISDOM OF BRUCE LEE

CHAPTERS

	ABOUT THE KFM ARCHIVE SERIES	13
	THE WISDOM OF BRUCE LEE The Enigma of the Lost Bruce Lee Book	17
	AN INTERVIEW WITH ROGER HUTCHINSON	21
01	THE FIGHTING MIND The Philosophy Of Kung Fu	35
02	THE MARTIAL ARTS ESTABLISHMENT The Classical Mess	47
03	NOT ONE, BUT ALL Jeet Kune Do Is Born	59
04	A FINGER POINTING AT THE MOON: On Training And Keeping Fit	73
05	I CAN GIVE YOU THE TOOLS The Teacher And The Student	85
06	HOW TO MEASURE YOUR OPPONENT Just How Good Are You?	97
07	FILM AND REALITY The Fighter As Actor And Director	107
08	THE HOLLYWOOD HERO Dynasties And Dragons	123
09	SWEET IMPRISONMENT Success And Stardom	131
10	THE HIDDEN MAN On Himself, Life and Truth	143
	BIBLIOGRAPHY & PHOTO CREDITS	165

KUNG-FU MONTHLY

THE ARCHIVE SERIES
ABOUT THE SERIES

THE WISDOM OF BRUCE LEE

Kung-Fu Monthly is a name synonymous with Bruce Lee, not only in the United Kingdom but throughout the world. It is a legend in its own right and a brand immediately recognisable by not only the font but also the famous "flying man" logo.

The popularity of the magazine at the peak of the Kung Fu Craze in the 1970s was unrivalled and its success was almost entirely down to pure luck.

Legend has it that *Kung-Fu Monthly* began life as a gamble by underground comic book publisher Felix Dennis after questioning a queue of kids outside a Soho cinema, waiting to see *Enter the Dragon* in early 1974. On paper, the idea seemed to serve the then-current trend of Bruce Lee and was deemed to have a shelf life of three to six months but a year after its launch, *Kung-Fu Monthly* had become the biggest-selling Bruce Lee magazine in the world.

After the demise of the Official Bruce Lee Fan Club in 1976, *Kung-Fu Monthly* launched their own. The KFM Bruce Lee Society ran for thirty quarterly newsletters from 1976 to 1983 and at the time of closing, had seen over five thousand eager Bruce Lee fans become members throughout its tenure, with the formidable Pam Hadden at the forefront throughout its seven active years.

Kung-Fu Monthly and The Bruce Lee Society were jointly responsible for the UK's first Bruce Lee Convention held on May 19th 1979 and the first Bruce Lee Film Festival held on December 1st 1979.

Kung-Fu Monthly and later *Personal Computer World*, had turned H. Bunch Associates from an underground publisher on the verge of bankruptcy to a publishing powerhouse, eventually becoming Dennis Publishing, named after its founder, Felix Dennis.

That leads us to today.

In February 2021, I approached Dennis Publishing with an idea for a project that I'd thought of doing for many years - scan, convert, edit and compile all seventy-nine issues of the iconic *Kung-Fu Monthly* magazine into book form, in order to present it to a new audience, as well as preserve its place in history.

It was the longest-running dedicated Bruce Lee magazine of its kind anywhere in the world (by frequency and circulation) and I wanted to pay homage to that. Such was its success and popularity that it was licensed throughout the world; in fourteen countries and in eleven languages. That doesn't even take into account the non-official bootlegs which appeared in China and Turkey. Nothing has matched it before or since. It truly has stood the test of time and having done so, has reached legendary status.

Kung-Fu Monthly is a snapshot of a time long gone; a time which the original fans remember with fondness and a time which new fans will hopefully discover.

The *Kung-Fu Monthly Archive Series* is dedicated to Felix Dennis and everyone associated with the magazine; not just the staff but also the fans, who would buy copies of the magazines in their millions over its lifetime and help cement the publication's place in British Pop Culture history.

Special thanks must also go to Carlotta Serantoni at Dennis Publishing for her assistance in allowing this project to go ahead.

Carl Fox
February 2022

KUNG-FU MONTHLY

THE ARCHIVE SERIES
THE WISDOM OF BRUCE LEE

THE ENIGMA OF THE LOST KFM BOOK

THE WISDOM OF BRUCE LEE

Around late 1976 and early 1977, two issues - numbers 19 and 20 - of the bizarrely popular *Kung-Fu Monthly* magazines, featured a two-part article on a new book from the magazine publishers entitled *The Wisdom of Bruce Lee*. For the first time, a publication looked into the art of Bruce Lee, which he called Jeet Kune Do and his philosophies on training in martial arts. This looked to be a totally revealing book on areas that, at that time, not been covered in any depth. All the fans at that time were totally engaged in getting this book to learn more about Bruce Lee's Kung Fu and not just his film work and personal life.

Then the strangest thing happened; it was never released in the UK, the home of *Kung-Fu Monthly*. Questions were asked throughout the life of the magazine and the newsletters of its fan club, The Bruce Lee Society, but nothing was ever resolved.

Then, years later, I discovered the book had actually been released in America in paperback format but not in the usual 8.5" x 11" format which *Kung-Fu Monthly* has established back in the day. Of course, I read it and was totally blown away by its content; it had been researched well and pre-dated any other book of its type on Bruce Lee by years.

Fast-forward forty-five years later to 2021. After the success of his KFM Bruce Lee Society newsletter book, compiler and editor Carl Fox approached Dennis Publishing, the copyright holder of *Kung-Fu Monthly*, to see if he could release the cannon of *Kung-Fu Monthly* magazines and books in a series of limited edition collector's books and surprisingly, they said, "Yes."

As soon as Carl told me of his new project, I immediately told him of the enigma of

The Wisdom of Bruce Lee. Of course, Carl knew nothing at that time about this book never being published in the UK. After a little research, it was found out that not only had it been published as a small paperback in the US, but it had also been published in the traditional *Kung-Fu Monthly* book format in The Netherlands, Germany and Italy in their respective languages.

Why it was never printed in the UK still seems to be an enigma, although it is known

THE KUNG-FU MONTHLY ARCHIVE SERIES

that the publisher, Felix Dennis, did move to America around early 1977 and perhaps signed an exclusivity deal with Pinnacle Publishing.

I am pleased to report that thanks to Carl Fox's tenacity and skills, he has put together two versions of this interesting and revealing book.

Firstly, an abridged version set out in the style of the other Kung-Fu Monthly books, so original collectors can complete their *Kung Fu Monthly* collection in their original format alongside other publications of the day such as The Book of Kung Fu, The Secret Art of Bruce Lee, The Power of Bruce Lee, Bruce Lee in Action, The Unbeatable Bruce Lee, King of Kung Fu and Who Killed Bruce Lee?

A second Deluxe version is the compete book with extras like the reprints from the original promotional articles that appeared in *Kung-Fu Monthly* No. 20 and 21, an interview with original author Roger Hutchinson and all photographs which appeared in the US paperback and European releases of the book.

I have to say this book would NEVER have been available in the UK without the sheer determination of Carl Fox and his dream to make these magazines and books available to fans at an affordable price to preserve their place in British history.

As it stands, part of the enigma has now been resolved but as to why it was never released in the UK after so much publicity at the peak of the Kung Fu Craze, that may never be resolved.

However, it just leaves me to say a big thank you to Carl - I hope everyone else appreciates your hard work.

Andrew Staton
October 2021

KUNG-FU
MONTHLY

THE ARCHIVE SERIES
THE WISDOM OF BRUCE LEE

AN INTERVIEW WITH ROGER HUTCHINSON

THE WISDOM OF BRUCE LEE

Born in 1949, Roger Hutchinson is an award-winning author and journalist from Farnworth in Lancashire. After leaving school in the late 1960s, he attended Bretton Hall College near Barnsley and Wakefield to study English. Whilst in his final year at Bretton Hall College, he founded and edited *Sad Traffic* - later becoming alternative newspaper, *STYNG* (*Sad Traffic Yorkshire News & Gossip*) - from a small office in Barnsley. After meeting Felix Dennis in London, he moved to the capital to work with him on *Oz*, *International Times* and *Time Out*, later becoming a freelance journalist.

After relocating to Skye, Hutchinson joined the *West Highland Free Press*. He is currently a feature journalist, columnist and reviewer for the *WHFP*, *The Scotsman*, *The Herald*, *The Guardian* and *The Press & Journal*. He has won several awards, including North of Scotland Feature Writer of the Year and UK Weekly Sports Writer of the Year.

He has also served as editor of the *Stornoway Gazette* and as of 2017, Hutchinson has written fifteen non-fiction books on subjects as diverse as the professional tennis circuit, The Royal Family, Sir Alf Ramsey, Bruce Lee and man-eating sharks.

His 1990 book *Polly: The True Story Behind Whisky Galore*, was shortlisted for The Royal Society of Literature's Ondaatje Prize.

He currently lives on the island of Raasay.

In March 2021, *Jun Fan Journal* writer Andrew Staton interviewed the accomplished author on his time working for Felix Dennis on his lesser-known book *The Wisdom of Bruce Lee*.

Roger Hutchinson with one of his favourite books, *Calum's Road*. Photograph Courtesy of Roger Hutchinson.

Why did you pick Bretton Hall near Barnsley to study English at College?

The college had a great reputation in 'arty' circles in the 60's. It had only been planned in the 40's as an arts college and eventually it became to focus more on drama but it had a good reputation before it started issuing teaching certificates. My father was a liberal educationalist and he suggested it to me. I had never heard of it and it was pretty difficult to get into a university at the time I was planning to go. I wasn't sure my A-Levels would have done it to get on the course or the place that I wanted. So Bretton Hall was the next best thing and you could do degree work there if you wanted. So I opted to study English and it was fantastic; just a great place to go.

With the location of Bretton Hall, it seems you eventually worked in Barnsley. How did that come about?

Well that came about because that's where I lived in my last year at Bretton and some friends of mine, some other students had a small house in Barnsley. It was a three-floor terrace house and we rented all three floors of it. It was myself, Richard Keys (who became an artist and was on the arts course at the same time as me) and other friends in the middle floor and on the bottom floor as well. Before we left college, we played around and brought out a small arts magazine called *Sad Traffic*, named after the Brian Patten poem. So when we left college we decided to bring out a newsletter which became *STYNG*, a regular paper or as regular as we could make it and so, that's what we did.

How did you end up going down to London to work?

It was a straight transfer. When doing our *STYNG* newsletter, we would take it down to London with us and drop a few hundred copies off there for sale. So, while we were down there, we got to know people and particularly the people who ran *Oz* magazine. I became friendly with some of the people from the magazine and it was the time of the *Oz* trial in 1970. We only went down to London two or three times a year to drop off copies of our magazine or should say I did. Slowly we found it hard to keep things going because we could not get much advertising, but the sales were good as far as we could gather. Getting the money back from the cover price was hellish and we realised that we did not know what we were doing. We knew nothing about publishing, and it was a very steep learning curve. It was difficult to keep it going, pay the printers bills and we did not know what to do. Then out of nowhere on New Year's Eve 1970/71, I got a telegram in Barnsley from Felix Dennis, asking me to ring him and so I did. He said Richard and Jim couldn't come back to the magazine after the trial as they were both burnt out and had gone to Australia, but he wanted to keep running it. He asked if I would go down to London and help him out.

So, was your first job working for Felix on Oz Magazine?

It was, without a question of a doubt and we brought out *Oz* throughout 1971. However, there were problems with one of the owners called Richard. He was in Australia and didn't want to do the magazine but wasn't sure he wanted anyone else doing it. He and

THE WISDOM OF BRUCE LEE

Felix never got on too great, so Felix was having a lot of trouble there. Meanwhile I was settling into London life and meeting up with new friends, as well as old ones. Two really good friends of mine, Nick Furan and Ed Barker were giving up editing the magazine *IT (International Times)* so the rest of the crew of *IT* asked me if I would jump ship from *Oz* and edit *IT*. So, I spoke to Felix about it who said that he could not guarantee what would happen with *Oz* and sure enough, it folded not long after. I quite fancied *IT* because it was regular fortnightly magazine. So, I went to *IT* where I worked for two years but then, all the underground press imploded. I went to *Time Out* for a while and then other magazines. *Friends Inc*, *Oz* and *International Times* were the last magazines to go, falling one after another and the writers left for *N.M.E* and *Melody Maker*. The time for those underground magazines was finished.

When did you start work on International Times?

I think it was about late 1971. I went down to work on *Oz* Magazine in January 1971, where I wrote for most of the year with Felix and it was in the summer or autumn when Felix was discovering he would not be able to bring *Oz* out anymore, as he and Richard Adams had a falling out. It was Richard's magazine, although he was no longer interested in it. It soon became apparent that it was all falling apart, and even though Felix never said I should find somewhere else to work, it was becoming clear to me that there was not going to be much of a future with the magazine. Nicky and Edward were leaving as editors of *International Times* and I knew that because we were all good friends. So, I was chatting to other people about moving over to this other magazine and I think it was the autumn, going into winter when I moved over to *IT*. I could honestly identify the first issue I was editor on.

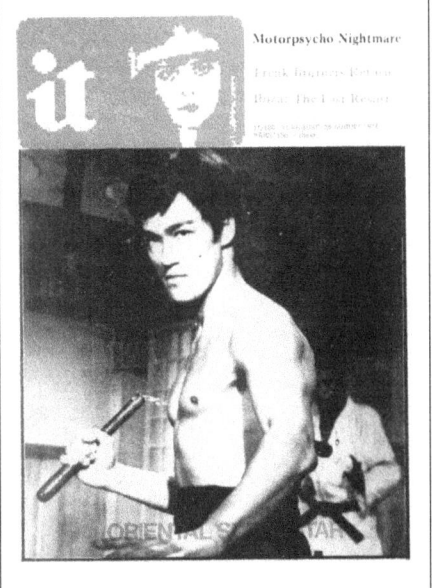

Do you remember editing an issue of International Times that came out in August 1973 with a Bruce Lee cover and if so, can you remember why you ran with that particular cover?

I can't really remember doing them but I do remember the covers. At the time, the magazine was busy and hard work. There were not many of us working on the magazine and we brought out a lot of issues. I wasn't really aware that we did the Bruce Lee issue before Felix did *Kung-Fu Monthly* though. *IT* was a current affairs magazine as much as it was anything and so the Bruce Lee phenomenon was something we had to try and reflect. With this issue having a Bruce Lee cover and not in a non-intestinal way, it may have been this magazine that Felix saw the saleability of Bruce Lee.

Was the writer of the Bruce Lee article in International Times No.160 called David Jenkins and did you know him?

Yes, David was the writer of that piece and I knew him very well indeed. We are still in touch and he is still around in London somewhere.

How did you meet and get to know Don Atyeo, who would go on to co-author the first Bruce Lee book Bruce Lee King of Kung Fu with Felix Dennis?

Don was around when I was editing *IT* in the early 70's. He came to our offices and asked if he could contribute to the magazine. He was a young Australian journalist, who had just arrived in London, and we got on very well, plus he was a really gifted and really talented journalist. He became a regular contributor to *IT* and then later on, after *IT* folded, Don was one of my journalists that went on to work for Felix, who he became really close to and worked with for many years. Actually, after working on *IT* and working for Felix, Don became editor of *Time Out* magazine which was a job that I did briefly but Don did it for much longer, I think, maybe a couple of years .Then he went off to Hong Kong to become an editor on a English language radio station which he made enough money out of to retire to his Uncle's old place along with his long term partner in rural France, where they still reside today.

The second Issue of International Times that you put Bruce Lee on the cover, it linked Bruce Lee to football, which was a very quirky little thing that nobody else had thought about. That was the June/July 1974 issue. Can you remember what sales were like for that issue at that time and did you sell more with Bruce on the cover?

Oh, I think we sold about 10,000 or 12,000 copies, but did we sell more because of a Bruce Lee cover? I don't really have those figures. There would have had to be a really big increase of sales before he got back to us. The sales would have had to have doubled or something but the distributors didn't come back to us to say that it was a top seller.

In the second issue of IT with Bruce Lee on the cover, it says Don Atyeo is the editor of that issue and the real editor (ie you) is in hiding. What was going on there?

I think I was on holiday for that issue and Don stood in for that issue and others if I or they were away.

Would it have been you or Don Atyeo who decided to put Bruce Lee on the cover of IT the second time?

We would have done it together. The magazines were prepared quite a long way in advance as it took quite a lot of time to prepare, and I would have gone on holiday for three weeks. Don Atyeo and Richard Adams, the designer, who also worked for Felix at a later stage, would have put the final touches to the magazine. I seem to remember that Edward, the other designer and I, were on holiday together on that particular occasion.

When you were editing IT, was it an in-house joke to change your names if you had written an article?

Yes, we used to do it all the time for a bit of fun.

What happened to Felix Dennis after the demise of the underground magazine scene?

Felix was not about to stop publishing, so he started out publishing comics and other things, expanding very quickly. He had an eye for talent in all fields and trends - that kind of thing. He started Bunch Books and employed a lot of his underground press colleagues and friends to do projects which not only helped us with our bills but it also helped him. By then, we were all very professional and we had learnt quickly in the underground press. So, a lot of us helped Felix; Richard Adams, Dick Fountain, Edward, Nicky, and before we knew it, Felix was publishing books. He was absolutely fascinated with Bruce Lee and he got everybody onto Bruce Lee as soon as he had seen one of the films. He said, "You've got to see this – it's completely different. This guy is the wave of the future." We had heard of Bruce Lee and he was taking the London Cinemas by storm but most of the established media thought it was beneath them and they were not interested. We were used to that kind of attitude from the established media, so it meant nothing to us. Felix saw a huge hole in the market here and wanted to start publishing things on this guy because he was an absolute phenomenon. With that, he started *Kung-Fu Monthly* and later, the Bruce Lee Society Fan Club - all sorts of stuff like that and that was the foundation of his printing organisation for quite a few years.

The first dummy issue of Kung-Fu Monthly that was sent to distributors as a test issue to see what they thought of the idea had the same image you used on the first Internation-

al Times with Bruce on the cover from August 1973. Did you know this and do you feel Felix may have been influenced by your Bruce Lee issues of IT to do Kung-Fu Monthly?

It's very possible because he would have certainly seen *IT* without a shadow of a doubt. He would have seen it and read it, not just because I was doing it, but because he had been reading it all his life. So, he may have seen it, loved it and been inspired to take it further. I don't really know for certain but it is quite possible.

Whilst working with Felix, do you remember someone called Bruce Sawford?

Yes, I remember Bruce Sawford, however I personally never worked with him. He was one of Felix's full time *Kung-Fu Monthly* staff on Goodge Street and had been at school with Felix. He was a super nice guy and a great guy to hang out with, chat to and go for a drink with.

Did you ever meet Pam Hadden, the president of the Bruce Lee Society?

Yes I did meet her once, but only briefly.

Can you remember how Felix and Don Atyeo got together?

Well even though I had left Felix, he still brought out a couple of issue of *Oz* before it folded in 1973, and Don and I helped with the magazine. We both contributed to his magazine, and Don and Felix got on very well from the start which continued on to Felix's own publishing business. I can categorically state that Don was involved with the last couple of issues of *Oz*.

Do you remember Felix and Don writing the Bruce Lee, The King of Kung Fu?

Oh yes. I remember that and in fact, I used it for research for my book, *The Wisdom of Bruce Lee*. They also did a book on Muhammad Ali, however as with my book for him, Felix put his name on the books as co-author. My book was all my own work and Don's book was all his own work.

So, where did the idea for Wisdom of Bruce Lee come from and did you write for Kung-Fu Monthly?

No, I didn't write for *Kung-Fu Monthly* but I did write the book you mentioned. As for whose idea it was, it was definitely Felix who came up with the idea, without a shadow of a doubt.

What drove you and inspired you to write such an outstanding book for its time on Bruce Lee?

Fascination of the research material I pulled together, and some my other better books have come out of that, and without that, you're advised not to start.

So how were you chosen to write the book for Felix, and was it written with Felix?

I wrote the book by myself but as to why he chose me, you would have to have asked Felix. I think he liked me because I was good at research, was a descent writer and I was interested.

Was Wisdom of Bruce Lee your first book or had you done several before?

No, I had never written before. Wisdom of Bruce Lee was my first book ever and since then, I have written twenty or so on various subjects.

The Wisdom of Bruce Lee is one of the best books from Bunch Books' cannon of literature on Bruce Lee as it deals with Lee's art and philosophies on Jeet Kune Do, being the first book of its type to do so. What source material did you use?

Wow! Now you're asking. It's a long time ago. These days you just go online and source your information from there but back then in the 1970's there was nothing like that. So, I just got everything I could from any and every resource at my disposal. I probably only used half of what I got but it got the job done. I picked out what I could use and just immersed myself in the subject at hand. As for the tone of the book, I am quite flattered and pleased with what you have said. Although it was a money-making exercise, it was enjoyable to do, and I remember that Felix liked it. On Bruce Lee himself, I was so stricken with sadness as it was a real pity that he died so young, not least because we never got to see what he would have developed into. I feel that he remains a bit of an enigma; I mean, nobody to this day could get to the bottom of what he was truly about. Had he survived, I think we would have learnt quite a lot more and it's just a crying shame on all levels.

Do you remember using Lee's Tao of Jeet Kune Do for your research?

Yes, I can remember the book and in fact, I think I still have a copy.

Do you know why your book, The Wisdom of Bruce Lee, was never released in the UK?

I'm not sure. I moved up to Scotland in 1977 and was writing a book about tennis, but I thought it got printed.

It did get printed in America and in some countries in Europe but not in the UK.

Ah well, Felix moved his publishing company to the US around that time and was running his publishing company from both New York and London, so I can only assume that he put it out in America to establish his business when he moved there. As for the absence of the book in the UK, I honestly do not know.

Speciale editie Kung-Fu. F. Dennis en R. Hutchinson.

Do you remember Felix calling himself Felix Yen for Kung-Fu Monthly and did you keep the research material you used for The Wisdom of Bruce Lee?

Yes, now you mention it, I remember Felix calling himself that silly name. That went back to our underground press days. As for the research material, I have kept it and its up in the loft somewhere I think.

Sadly, Felix Dennis isn't around anymore. What was it like to work with him?

Felix Dennis was one of the most outstanding talents to come out of the underground press. I would like to say that the underground press had some very talented people working for it, from likes of Germaine Greer, Marian Miles and Ed Barker plus various colleagues. Richard Neville, who founded *Oz* in Australia and then in London, was an amazing talent and a unique individual. Felix was the same in his own way. As you know, Felix was from South London and was so excited by *Oz*, he wangled a job on there. He then very quickly absorbed the publishing industry and everything about it. He became an absolute expert in no time at all and this included what was likely to be popular, what might sell, what might move. It was no accident that Felix became filthy rich. One of my first conversations with Felix was when I went down to the *Oz* magazine premises to say hello and to deliver some copies of *STYNG* down there as used the same distributer as *Oz* and *IT*. I went down to their base on Princeton Road, West London in 1970, just before the trial and these guys had a lot on their minds including being sent to jail. When I handed a couple of copies of *STYNG* to Felix, he went out of his way to be interested and curious. He was looking through a copy of *STYNG*, nodding approvingly, encouraging me, giving me a lesson on magazine design, and pointing out bits of *STYNG* that became so evident to me as part of what you did. I had this talk with Felix in the space of about 15 minutes on Princeton Road when really, he would have been far better spending his time preparing his defence for the Old Bailey. His aptitude for publishing was a phenomenon - an absolute phenomenon. I have often thought that with all the talents that I have worked with - let alone the ones that came before from the underground press, particularly from *IT* and *Oz* - if all that talent had come together and worked under Felix in just one magazine, it could have been one hell of a magazine.

After writing your first book on Bruce Lee, you have gone on to write twenty or so more books. Which out of these did you enjoy the most and get the most out of writing?

Well it would have to be one of the Highland books, probably Poole or Calum's Road. They have also been two really big sellers. In hindsight, I really enjoyed writing both of those.

As a Footnote to this interview, it can be seen that Roger Hutchinson was maybe the first person to put Bruce Lee on the cover of a magazine in the UK. His creativity was most likely the inspiration to Felix Dennis prior to the creation of Kung-Fu Monthly. He was the person responsible for bringing Don Atyeo onto the scene and later into the Kung-Fu Monthly equation. He also wrote the first book to demonstrate the Chinese philosophical thinking of Bruce Lee.

If you get to read the first International Times with Bruce Lee on the cover, you will realise that in London in 1973, the Bruce Lee phenomenon was starting, and International Times, prior to going to press, must have been in touch with Cathay Films and not Warner Brothers, as there is no mention of Enter The Dragon in David Jenkins' article. However he does talk about all of Bruce Lee's Hong Kong Mandarin films he made for Golden Harvest, which included Big Boss, Fist of Fury, Way of the Dragon and surprisingly, Game of Death, the last film incomplete project he was working on at that time. International Times No.160 is a time capsule to the birth of the Bruce Lee legacy in the United Kingdom, acting as a precursor to the legendary Kung-Fu Monthly. Without a doubt, Roger Hutchinson, unknowingly was the man that started a tribute to Bruce Lee that has lasted to today, and will continue to do so.

Andrew Staton and Carl Fox
October 2021

KUNG-FU
MONTHLY

THE ARCHIVE SERIES
THE WISDOM OF BRUCE LEE

CHAPTER ONE

THE FIGHTING MIND
The Philosophy of Kung Fu

"A Kung Fu man employs his mind as a mirror - it grasps nothing, and it refuses nothing. It receives, but does not keep. Let the mind think what it likes without interference by the separate thinker or ego within oneself. So long as it thinks what it wants, there is absolutely no effort in letting it go; and the disappearance of the effort to let it go is precisely the disappearance of the separate thinker."

- BRUCE LEE

THE FIGHTING MIND
The Philosophy of Kung Fu

"A Kung Fu man employs his mind as a mirror - it grasps nothing, and it refuses nothing. It receives, but does not keep. Let the mind think what it likes without interference by the separate thinker or ego within oneself. So long as it thinks what it wants, there is absolutely no effort in letting it go; and the disappearance of the effort to let it go is precisely the disappearance of the separate thinker."

- BRUCE LEE

There is a form of Chinese verse and philosophical truism whose sole basis is the description of one or more facets of "the superior man." Thus, Confucius was led to write: "If the superior man abandons virtue, how can he fulfil the requirements of that name?"

The equally respected Lao Tzu commented that: "The superior man anticipates tasks that are difficult while they are still easy, and does things that would become great while they are small. Therefore, the superior man, while he never does what is great, is able on that account to accomplish the greatest of things."

If all of these statements and snippets were amalgamated, and if some human creature found himself capable of fulfiling each and every one of them, then the result would not only be a paragon of every human virtue. It would also be a walking definition of the term "Kung Fu."

It is Westerners who have been guilty of bastardising the meaning of Kung Fu, adopting it as a phrase-like "Karate" - meaning simply some deadly form of fighting skill. Nothing could be further from the truth. Kung Fu, according to its original Chinese translation, is an accomplishment, a skill, a perfection of one or many arts. A master of Kung Fu would be well versed in philosophy, an able alchemist, knowledgeable in practical medicine, an entertaining musician, thoroughly read in verse and prose and finally, able to defend himself and others against attack. To view his accomplishment in the Martial Arts as paramount is to mistake the purpose of his calling, and to see the nature of Kung Fu in a false light.

But man is an aggressive, violent animal, impressed more by strength of body and speed of limb than by some pithy muse. Perhaps it was inevitable that the martial facet of Kung Fu should come to eclipse the rest. Legend and myth have added their weight to this process; even today, the Kung Fu Sifu of ancient China is portrayed in contemporary books and stories as a symbol of native insurrection against oppression - a kind of Asian Robin Hood. Certainly it is true that such institutions as Shaolin monasteries were often forced into postures of reluctant resistance by the folly and cruelty of China's past rulers.

It was the emperor's repressive decree forbidding peasants or travellers to carry arms which did much to foster the spread and popularity of systems of unarmed combat. Later, it has to be said, the Martial Arts were used in a more provocative manner by the instigators of the Boxer Rebellion (whose misinterpretation of their inherited skills also led them to believe that the white man's bullets could not harm a Kung Fu master), and over the last fifty years the dual onslaught of movies (particularly those produced by the Hong Kong "Mandarin" film industry) and television (such as Warner Bros.' Kung Fu) has succeeded in dissociating the term Kung Fu from all of its traditional meanings but the one which suggests prowess in the Martial Arts.

The nature of Kung Fu, however, is such that it demands of an expert practitioner rather more than quick reflexes and efficient muscles. When Bruce Lee said that the Martial Arts are about self-knowledge, he was echoing the comment of Lao Tzu that: "A skilful warrior strikes a decisive blow and stops. He does not continue his attack to assert his mastery. He will strike the blow, but be on his guard against being vain or arrogant over his success. He strikes it as a matter of necessity, but not from a wish of mastery."

In other words, the qualities necessary to perfect the art of Kung Fu include humility, restraint, and all those virtues that culture teaches. Without such virtues, it is not possible to become a competent Martial Artist. Indeed, students from the Shaolin temple were not allowed to leave the monastery until they had passed a series of tests designed to assess their various qualities - from questions on philosophy and history to the more strenuous "running the gauntlet" of more than a hundred armed and mechanized dummies, and the celebrated final test of endurance, the lifting of a red-hot heavy metal urn away from the exit. One pupil actually did succeed in leaving the monastery without passing these last two tests. Hu Wei-ch'uan escaped through the sewers after fifteen years - and we should be glad that he did, for after the Manchus had destroyed the Shaolin temples Hu Wei-ch'uan was one of the few survivors able to pass on the secrets of his teachings.

There are two broad philosophies of Kung Fu, two distinct "schools," which are usually referred to as the "hard" school and the "soft" school, or the "external" school and the "internal" school. Into each of these categories falls a plethora of substyles, each with a different origin and philosophy.

The external styles were taught initially at the Shaolin temples. Months, even years, would be spent preparing the body for preliminary training in such styles. The student would be obliged to take up the strenuous "horse stance" for hours at a time, thus gradually lowering his centre of gravity and basically learning how to stand. And the student would also learn to develop that mystical quality: the power of chi. John F. Gilbey, in his fascinating book *Secret Fighting Arts of the World*, claims to have witnessed two startling examples of chi. Gilbey says he saw the legendary Chinese master Chou Hsu-lai (whose name was so awe-inspiring in pre-revolutionary China that companies would pay him to allow them to write on the side of their goods-trucks that Chou was giving them protection) jump from a third-story window to the ground beside the watching Gilbey, unhurt and without making the slightest noise.

Some years later, Gilbey met the Japanese master Junzo Hirose. Hirose demonstrated his powers in the following exchange: "Have you practiced kendo?' he asked.

"When I told him I was only second-grade black belt in the sport, he laughed, 'That is certainly enough to know how to swing a sword.' Then he asked me to strike with all my strength at his left forearm. He enjoined me to focus well since, if I hit his upper arm inadvertently, it would be unfortunate.

"I took the sword from the assistant, focused on Hirose's arm, and brought the sword down sharply. I could exaggerate and say I used all my strength. In truth, I did not. I was afraid that if I used everything my focus might be disturbed and I might hit his upper arm. So I used controlled power.

"No half-arm fell on the floor. No blood spurted. Hirose did not scream or faint. In an unbelieving trance I held his arm and gazed at it. A red line creased the skin, but that was all. The master gestured us to be seated again."

Such power cannot be learned by hours of weight-lifting or routine drills in a gymnasium. They are half-spiritual abilities, gained as much by meditation and lengthy reflection as by physical exercise. Gilbey recommends an elementary method of "laying in a store

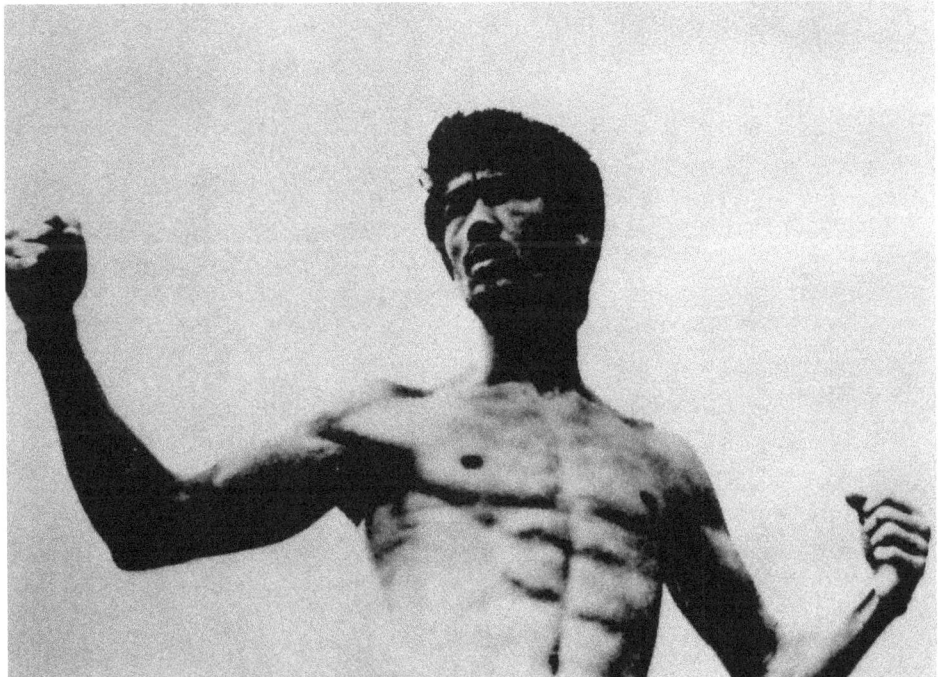

of chi."

The student should find a quiet, secluded place, and sit there comfortably. Having relaxed, he should then take care to breathe in through the nose and out through the mouth, slowly. Then the right ear should be covered gently with the palm of the left hand, and the left ear with the palm of the right hand. This exercise should last for fifteen minutes, and should be repeated daily. Thus would novice monks at the Shaolin temple be initiated into the elementary skills of Kung Fu.

The various styles which were taught to individual students of the external school were more specific in origin and purpose. Perhaps the most celebrated is the "Preying Mantis" style, which was developed in the middle ages, according to legend, by a swordsman who found himself unable to beat any Shaolin monk in combat, because of his own inadequate schooling. This swordsman, Wang Lang, then decided, in the words of the poet Chi K'ang: "I will cast out Wisdom and reject Learning. My thoughts shall wander in the Great Void."

While wandering, literally, in the "great void" of central China, Lang observed a slender, small preying mantis doing battle with a much bulkier grasshopper. The preying mantis, by careful use of its claw-like front feet, turned out the winner.

Lang subsequently caught many of the insects, and by feeding them, and forcing them into battle with various foes, learned their method of attack and defence, and adapted it to the human form. On returning to Shaolin, he was able to defeat all comers,

and instantly became a hero of the Martial Arts, for as Chang Chao has said: "A cultured man who does not rest with his smug opinions has something of the conqueror's spirit."

That same great philosopher, Chang Chao, has also said that, "A small injustice can be drowned by a cup of wine; a great injustice can be drowned only by the sword." There are those who would differ, pointing to the Drunkard's style. This eccentric form of the external Martial Arts speaks for itself; the practitioner would wobble, stagger, and slew about, disconcerting his opponent, and above all, being totally unpredictable. It is a more effective style than might be supposed. John Gilbey tells of a South African farmer who had probably never heard of the Shaolin temple, but had certainly mastered the elements of the Drunkard's style.

This farmer challenged Gilbey (himself an accomplished fighter) to a no-holds-barred encounter. Gilbey accepted, and set about his man. The farmer took little time to knock over, and soon lay unconscious on the ground. Gilbey dusted himself off, and walked over to his opponent, musing on what small effort it had taken to beat him. Gilbey bent over to see if the farmer was seriously hurt and felt a sudden, excruciating pain in the groin, where the farmer's boot had just landed. The pain grew so intense that Gilbey blacked out, and when he awoke the farmer had gone. But lying on the ground beside Gilbey was a slip of paper with one word on it. That word was surprise, and it is the key word of the Drunkard's style, whether practiced on the South African savannah or the Chinese plains. And it is very close to what Bruce Lee was talking about when he dismissed too many classical forms as being ritualised and predictable.

The "internal" or "soft" school of Martial Arts philosophy is characterized by a greater use of chi, and the expenditure of less apparent effort. That said, the value of many soft-school styles as actual fighting forms has been criticised - not least by Lee, who constantly demanded practicality and effectiveness. It is true that many a slow, stylised

Kata in the internal manner would be of little use in a street fight. But there are other advantages. The soft school of Kung Fu, with its emphasis on inner calm and the development of chi, is an immense medical aid, greatly beneficial to all inner organs - particularly the genitalia, the stomach and cardiovascular systems, and the nervous system. Such strengthening of the system, which is naturally of great value today, was of inestimably greater worth in ancient China, where any illness could easily be fatal, and was certainly dangerously debilitating. The poet Po-Chu'i expressed the almost hopeless state of being ill in a country without welfare: "I have been ill so long that I do not count the days; At the southern window, evening and again evening. Sadly chirping in the grasses under my eaves. The winter sparrows morning and evening sing. By an effort I rise and lean heavily on my bed."

Ancient Kung Fu masters were also necessarily skilful masseurs, herbalists, and acupuncturists - doctors of Chinese medicine. These are treatments for disease which Western medicine is only just learning to accept and acknowledge. For although many an old woman in the West may have handed down her rheumatic cure of squashed dandelion and parsnip, doctors in the West have consistently and coldly refused to entertain the idea that herbs have medical use.

Only when it began to transpire that such an herb as ma huang, the thousand-year-old Chinese cure for asthma actually contained ephedrine, which doctors in the West

prescribe for asthma, did the Western medical establishment have to take notice. Similarly, the ancient art of acupuncture, proven over the centuries to exert almost miraculous healing and anaesthetic powers, came into Kung Fu training years ago, and only recently became of interest to Western minds.

In massage, the Chinese based their teaching on the three meridians, linking all the major internal organs. Once the flow of these meridians through the body becomes understood, it is possible to massage in a manner strengthening to those major organs. The liver, for instance, could be stimulated into more effective action.

The various health-giving qualities of different schools of Martial Arts were of great consequence then, demonstrating once again the wide, catholic functions and purposes of Kung Fu.

It is the practitioners of internal styles of the Martial Arts that have been responsible for most of the unbelievable feats, the mystical, superhuman feats of strength, resistance, and delicate timing. If the external school is that of speed, strength, and efficiency, the internal school is of subtlety and hidden depths.

As Wang Chung-yueh described it: "The aim of tai chi is to sacrifice oneself to comply with an adversary. Yet many regard this as a mistake similar to abandoning the near to seek the far. This attitude could be correctly likened to making a mistake of a fraction of an inch and end up missing the target by a thousand miles. Therefore, in the study of the art, the wise student uses his discretion."

Those are the rules which Bruce Lee threw away. This book will contain enough of his own angular comment on the philosophies of the ancient Martial Arts, without including it in this introductory chapter. But it is worth pointing out that, in rebelling against the idealised, fixed conception of the Martial Arts, in demystifying the fighting skills, Lee was actually following in a long tradition of unorthodox fighters. There had not, it is true, been a figure as controversial and powerful as he for many years. But the great Martial Artists, such as the aforementioned Wang Lang, have always been innovators, regarded warily by their contemporaries. But in the same way that the Shaolin monks, having observed Wang's preying mantis style, begged him to teach them, so all over the world millions of people from all age groups, from all races and creeds, are attempting to emulate Bruce Lee's Martial Arts philosophy.

In the only book he ever wrote, *The Tao of Jeet Kune Do*, Lee made it clear that his road was not the easiest of ways. It is a trite assumption, commonly held, that the stripping down of styles into one effective form - which is the essence of Jeet Kune Do - might somehow be a quicker, painless way of accumulating fighting skills. In fact, Lee points out, the "formless form" is the most elevated state, and can only be achieved after mastery of a number of those "minor" forms which once were an end in themselves.

On top of this, Jeet Kune Do requires of its practitioners something which Lee feared was disappearing fast from the fighting arts - initiative, the ability to adapt to the unexpected, rather than simply work out with a time-worn and tired Kata. Lee was opposed (as were the old masters) to any frivolous idea of Kung Fu as a sport, or a game. It was a way of life or it was nothing. He believed (again, as did the old masters) that man was inherently weak in mind and pure at heart, and that the pursuit of the Martial Arts could strengthen the former and emphasise the latter.

But there were aspects of the Martial Arts and their traditional philosophies that made Lee uneasy. He once described himself as "mid-Pacific man," and this combination of Chinese and American culture brought about complications in him. This is probably clearest in his attitude towards Buddhism. The scepticism towards organized religion that America taught him bounced sharply back off his Eastern education. It was a complication that he seemed never to resolve; on the one hand he was capable of pointing out the Eight-fold Path of Buddha toward full knowledge and understanding of life, and on the other hand he could scathingly reject such mystical, religious notions. Part of him saw religion as a manifestation of man's desire to shrug the responsibility for his own life off onto some nebulous "force beyond man's control" as a weakness - and Lee despised weakness. And another part of him whispered that the great visions and truths of religious men were not to be lightly rejected, but were rather to be studied and absorbed, to be used selectively in the formation of man's character in the same way that the useful parts of other styles were accommodated in Jeet Kune Do.

Essentially, Lee was a pragmatist. He believed in making efficient use of the resources available to him, and therein lies the secret of his unique contribution to the Martial Arts philosophies. In less than a decade, he stripped away centuries of obfuscation; in a practical, straightforward manner that suddenly made sense, he pointed out that a punch was not a willow tree or a delicate spring shower, it was a punch and no more or less. If comparing it to a willow tree or a shower of rain helped a pupil to understand its nature and purpose, then well and good, but ultimately it should be recognised as something whose purpose was to stun or otherwise injure an opponent.

There are those who regret the influence that Bruce Lee has had on the Martial Arts, who would claim that what seems to be a revitalising and updating of an art form has actually corrupted it beyond repair, and there are those who would argue that Lee's was a false revolution, an exercise in publicity and the accumulation of fame and money rather than a necessary review of the meaning of the Martial Arts. Lee, the pragmatist, knew about such criticism, and rarely directly argued with it. His power and almost paranormal grace answered for him. Had he wished, however, Lee might have spoken of his effect on the Martial Arts in the words of Wu-Ti, who while an emperor of the Liang dynasty in ancient China, wrote a poem entitled *The Liberator*.

THE LIBERATOR

In the high trees - many doleful winds:
The ocean waters - lashed into waves.
If the sharp sword be not in your hand,
How can you hope that your friends will remain many ?
Do you not see that sparrow on the fence?
Seeing the hawk it casts itself into the snare.
The fowler to catch the sparrow is delighted:
The young man to see the sparrow is grieved.
He takes his sword and cuts through the netting:
The yellow sparrow flies away, away.
Away, away up to the blue sky
And down again to thank the Young Man.

- Wu-Ti

The netting of the old Martial Arts philosophies has been slashed beyond repair, and more people seem inclined to thank Bruce Lee for it than to criticise him.

THE WISDOM OF BRUCE LEE

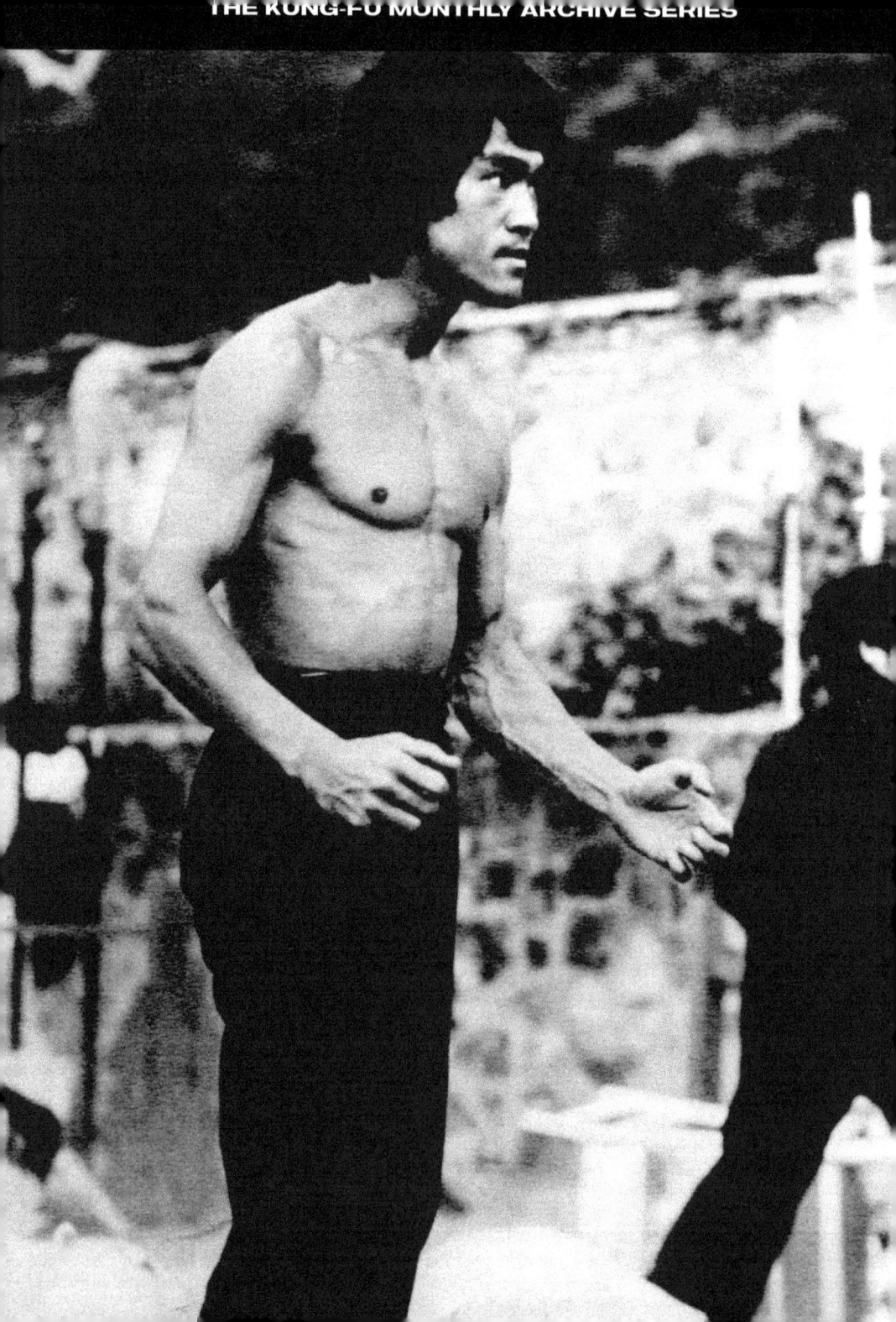

CHAPTER TWO

THE MARTIAL ARTS ESTABLISHMENT
The Classical Mess

> "True Kung Fu is rooted in the feet. It develops in the legs, is directed by the waist, and functions through the fingers."
>
> — CHANG SAN-FENG

THE MARTIAL ARTS ESTABLISHMENT
The Classical Mess

"True Kung Fu is rooted in the feet. It develops in the legs, is directed by the waist, and functions through the fingers."

- CHANG SAN-FENG

It seems unusual for a movie star actually to be competent in the art that he popularises on the screen. Roger Moore (James Bond), for instance, admits that he cannot fire a gun without flinching and closing his eyes; James Stewart confesses to having some difficulty riding horses; and Larry (Al Jolson) Parks couldn't sing to save his life. As the exception, Bruce Lee was more than merely competent at the Martial Arts. He was acknowledged as an international master.

Lee's knowledge of the subject was devastating. A whole room in his house was dedicated to books on the Martial Arts, reputedly the biggest fight library in the world.

Senator John Tunney, son of the famous boxer Gene Tunney, was having dinner with Lee one evening when Lee mentioned that he had read two books on fighting that Gene had written. John Tunney was astonished. He has never, before or since, met anybody who even knew that his father had written those books.

"As a kid in Hong Kong," Lee recalled, "I was a punk and went looking for fights. We used chains and pens with knives hidden inside. Then, one day, I wondered what would happen if I didn't have my gang behind me when I got into a fight. I decided to learn how to protect myself and I began to study Kung Fu."

From the very beginning of that training, Lee would have been made to realise that he was entering a calling with a long, distinguished, and well-recorded tradition. Without being particularly generous in estimations, it is possible to trace a disciplined form of Kung Fu back into history more than 2,500 years, immortalised in the words of Lao Tzu,

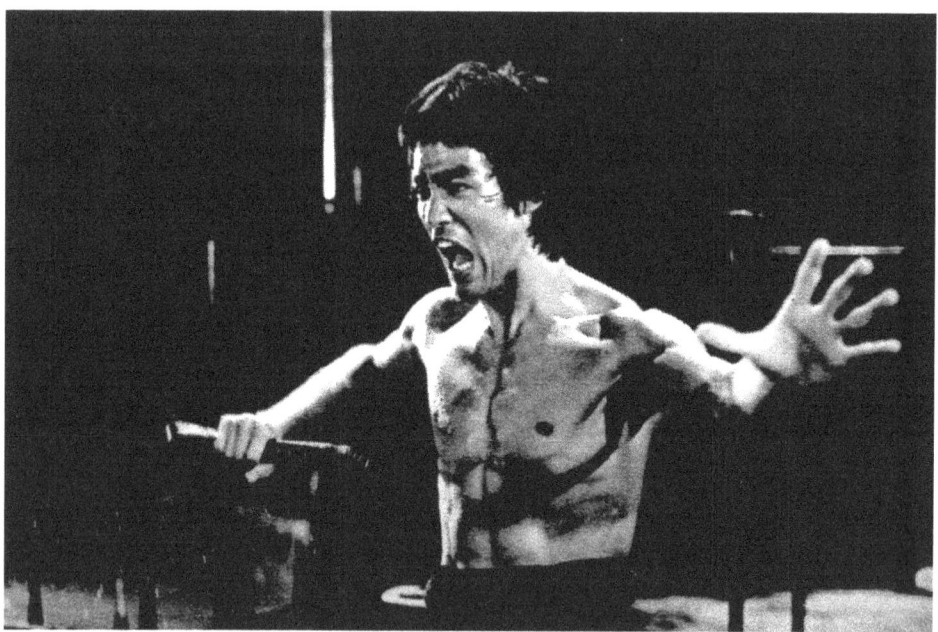

who knew enough to write: "A brave soldier is not violent. A skilful fighter does not lose his temper. A great general wins without a battle. A mighty ruler governs through humility. This is known as the Virtue of Not Striving."

Such merging of Taoist meditations and the act of physical combat really mark the beginning of Kung Fu. But it was a thousand years later, about 500 A.D. that an Indian Buddhist wandered with his spiritual teachings into wild, lawless China. This Buddhist, Bodhidharma, like some fighting street priest of later days, decided that it was more practical to teach his dispossessed, molested and hungry students the principles of unarmed combat, mixed healthily with spiritual well-being. The monks of the Shaolin temple to whom Bodhidharma imparted this knowledge, learned it well, and developed his groundwork as the centuries passed.

As a disrespectful street punk, Lee was entering fairly hallowed ground. He would have learned how, in Kansu province during the reign of Kubla Khan, Chuah Yuan witnessed an old and withered street trader being "mugged" by a massive thug. The attacker went to kick the veteran in the face, and the old man "pressed two fingers of his right hand against the out-flung boot. The attacker crumpled to the ground, unconscious." As a result of studying this old man's powers, Yuan was able to expand Bodhidharma's 18 basic movements into 170 movements, grouped into five schools. Lee came to know these schools, and to question their purpose more vitally than any other fighter for centuries. But as a teenager, he learned respect on that hallowed ground.

He threw himself into studying the Martial Arts at the Wing Chun School, under a respected master, Ip Man, whose individual attention Lee valued so much that he would stand outside the school before lessons waving the other students away, saying "No class today." He was studying Wing Chun because he felt it to be the most valuable Kung Fu style. He had mixed memories of the school: "I have to give the Japanese credit for installing regimentation in their schools. The Japanese Sensei (Teacher) is revered and his command is law; but not the Sifu (Kung-Fu Teacher). We used to address our Sifu with 'Hey, old man, what do you have in mind for us to do?' If we didn't like what he wanted us to do, we used to say, 'Goddamn it! We have to do that crap again?'"

Many of Lee's fellow punks dropped out. "They didn't take Kung Fu for health reasons, but just to learn to fight," he later sanctimoniously decided but Lee remained to share the thrills of battles between schools:
"Like the old tradition, one school would challenge another," he related, "and a designated place and time would be set. On the day of reckoning, both schools would have their instructors and students to cheer their fighter. Impromptu rules would be established, but those rules would be so minimal that the fight would be just about 'all out.' Nobody really got hurt because the arts weren't that effective. I never saw anybody really get hurt badly enough to be sent to the hospital."

Sent to the University of Washington to study philosophy, Lee's interest in the Martial Arts did not wane. Indeed, he occasionally used his academic course to explore his extracurricular interests, as in this essay that he wrote for an English course. It was titled "A Moment of Understanding," and in it Lee described Kung Fu as a special kind of skill, an art rather than physical exercise. The art is a subtle one of matching the mind's essence to that of the technique with which it has to work. The principle of Kung Fu is not exactly scientific, a thing that can be learned by fact-finding or instruction. Like a flower, it must grow spontaneously, in a mind free from emotion and desires. The core of this principle of Kung Fu is Tao - the spontaneity of the universe.

Four years of arduous training, in the art of Kung Fu taught Lee to understand the principle of gentleness - neutralising your opponent's effort and minimising your own expenditure of energy. The discipline lay in calmness and not striving.

The idea sounded simple, but actual application was difficult. The moment Lee engaged in combat with an opponent, he found that his mind was perturbed and emotions stirred up. After a series of blows and kicks, all the theory was gone. Lee's one remaining thought was somehow or another, he must beat his opponent.

Professor Ip, head of Wing Chun School, would come up to Lee, instructing him to relax and calm his mind. "Forget about yourself and follow the opponent's movement," he would say. "Let your mind do the counter-movement without deliberation. Learn the art of detachment."

That was the secret-to relax. But when Lee learned he must relax he was immediately up against a contradiction. The effort in "must" was inconsistent with the effortlessness of "relax." When Lee's self-consciousness grew to frustrating proportions, his instructor again approached him and said, "Lee, follow nature and don't interfere. Never assert yourself against nature: never be in opposition to any problem, but swing with it. Don't practice this week. Go home and think."

Lee stayed home the following week. After many hours of meditation, he gave up and decided to go sailing alone in a junk. At sea, the thought of his training made him mad at himself, and he punched at the water. At that moment the thought suddenly struck him that water, this very basic stuff, was the essence of Kung Fu. Didn't it illustrate the principle of Kung Fu? One could strike water, but it did not suffer damage. One could stab it, yet it would not be wounded. To grasp a handful of it was impossible. Water could fit into any shape of container, and although it seemed weak, it could eventually penetrate any substance in the world. The nature of water - that was what Lee discovered as a guiding principle.

Still savouring this experience, Lee continued to gaze into the water when suddenly a bird flew over, casting a reflection. Another hidden meaning seemed clarified. Shouldn't the thoughts and emotions that he had in front of an opponent pass like the reflection of a bird over the water? Lee felt that this was what Professor Ip meant by being detached - to accept by going with, and not against, one's nature.

Lee lay on the boat, feeling that he had united with tao, had become one with nature. Letting the boat drift freely, Lee just lay there, enjoying a state of inner feeling in which opposition had become mutually cooperative instead of mutually exclusive, in which there was no longer any conflict in his mind.

Later, he was to apply the lesson learned by his experience on the junk to his own friends and students, having rationalised the state of tao, and become convinced that technical knowledge of Kung Fu did not make a man its master. The spirit of Kung Fu could be grasped only when a man's mind was in harmony with the principle of life itself, that is, when he attained a state known in Taoism as "no-mindedness." This consists in preserving absolute fluidity of the mind, keeping it free from all intellectual considerations and affective disturbances. According to Lee's belief, everybody can think himself into his goal if he mixes his thoughts with persistence, definition of purpose, and an intense desire for its translation into reality.

By this time, Lee had decided what kind of a man he wanted to be. Given his training and upbringing, it cannot have been too difficult a decision.

He recognised that the world is full of people who are determined to be somebody or else. Such people want to get ahead, but ambition has no place in Kung Fu, whose students must reject all forms of self-assertiveness and competition. It should be pointed out that these ideas were expressed before the possibility of becoming a star crossed his mind, but however he may have changed, he wholeheartedly believed in such passivity.

Lee also felt that a Kung Fu man who was really good, was not proud at all. Pride emphasises the superiority of one's status. There has to be fear and insecurity in pride according to Lee's thinking, because when you aim at being highly esteemed and achieve such status, you automatically start to worry about losing status.

Lee felt that a Kung Fu man lives without being dependent on the opinion of others, and that a Kung Fu master, unlike the beginner, holds himself in reserve. He is quiet and unassuming, with no desire to show off. Kun Fu training creates a proficiency that becomes spiritual. The master is made freer through spiritual struggle. Fame and status means nothing to him.

These ideas show the gentle humble influence of old Professor Ip. But it was an influence that Lee came largely to reject, as his self-confidence and knowledge increased.

A later definition of "classical Kung Fu man" with the one previously noted shows his changing ideas. He came to feel that the "classical" man is just an assortment of routines, ideas, and traditions that lock him into a mould and prevent the self-expression and understanding that are essential to mastery. For Lee reality changed every minute, even as he said it.

His impatience with the classical arts knew few bounds. Where he had once written that there were two main Kung Fu schools, the "hard" and the "soft" school, elaborating their differences, he would later snap that it was an illusion. Gentleness/firmness were seen as one inseparable force of an unceasing interplay of movement. He felt that teachers who claimed that their styles were soft or hard clung blindly to one partial view of the totality.

And where once he had believed, along with almost every other Kung Fu practitioner in the world, that: "The application of the principles of Yin and Yang in Kung Fu are expressed as the Law of Harmony. It states that one should be in harmony with, not rebellion against, the strength and force of the opposition. When opponent A uses strength (Yang) on B, B must not resist him with strength; in other words do not use positiveness (Yang) against positiveness (Yang) but instead yield to him with softness (Yin) and lead him to the direction of his own force, negativeness (Yin) to positiveness (Yang)."

Later he came to mock such concepts: "I was once asked by a so-called Chinese Kung Fu 'Master' - one of those that really looked the part with beard and all - as to what I thought of Yin and Yang? I simply answered 'Baloney!' Of course, he was quite shocked at my answer and still has not come to the realisation that 'it' is never two."

Although it is a simple and obvious truth that Bruce Lee was not born to be a meek conformist, there was more to such rude dismissals of the old traditions than juvenile rebellion. Lee recognised that much of the ancient, textbook styles had become irrelevant, worthless, about as much use in training for combat as push-ups. As usual, he expressed such criticism concisely enough himself, in *Black Belt* magazine: "Too much horsing around with unrealistic stances and classical forms and rituals. It's just too artificial and mechanical and doesn't really prepare a student for actual combat. A guy could get clobbered while getting into his classical mess. Classical methods like these, which I consider a form of paralysis, only solidify and condition what was once fluid. Their practitioners are merely blindly rehearsing systematic routines and stunts that will lead to nowhere."

Lee went on to say that in actual combat, you're fighting a living, moving object, who must be dealt with realistically. Indulging in unnecessary moves in a street fight will get you your shirt ripped off. When someone grabs you, punch him, and forget the non-functional fancy stuff. Lee then dismissed classical methods as "organized despair."

In his campaign to put the Martial Arts into a big bag, shake them up, and see what transpired when the bag was emptied, Lee succeeded in antagonising many people. It was to be expected. He did not mince words, and while his sharp condemnations of classical styles may have been necessary in the purging that he was convinced had to occur, they cannot have been pleasant for those on the receiving end. Even Ip Man would surely have shuddered to hear Lee say that the Chinese masters who say that their chi, or internal power, has sunk to their stomachs are not kidding; that they are nothing but fat and ugly.

His belief, incidentally, that the older masters had betrayed the art could have had something to do with a decision that he came to that a Martial Artist should retire from the public arena at forty-five: "The man himself will not realise it," he told a journalist, "but physiologically he is already on the decline, and I think the fighter over forty-five should sit back and watch the emergence of new fighters."

Or, still putting it bluntly: "Ninety-nine percent of the whole business of Oriental self-defence is baloney. It's fancy jazz. It looks good, but it doesn't work. If a ninety-pound woman is attacked by a two-hundred-and-fifty-pound man, the only thing she can do is strike hard at one of three places - the eyeballs, the groin, or the shins. This should be sufficient to put the man off-balance for just a moment, and then she'd better run like hell."

Lee thought that breaking bricks and boards with the edge of your hand was irrelevant, a gimmick. Martial Arts are about self-defence, and a brick or board would never instigate a fight. Similarly other Karate disciplines were more a hindrance than a help, because while you remembered what you'd been taught to do in a situation your opponent could kill you, which is exactly what you should be trying to do to him.

According to Lee, the majority of Martial Arts students are there only out of vanity. It is exotic. They figure they'll learn how to live a beautiful life through Zen and meditation. But Lee felt that if you want something beautiful, you should take up modern dancing. What good is it for a Boxer to learn to meditate? He's a fighter, not a monk. Besides, it's all too ritualistic. That sort of Oriental self-defence is like swimming on land, Lee said. You can learn the strokes, but if you're never in the water, it's nonsense.

He even turned his wit against that most honoured of Martial Arts totems: the "belt" system of grading ability. Asked what colour belt he himself owned, he replied: "I don't have any belt whatsoever. That is just a certificate. Unless you can really do it, that belt doesn't mean anything. I think it might be useful to hold your pants up, but that's about all."

The final insult, specifically designed to remove himself finally and irrevocably from the Martial Arts establishment, was the small tombstone near the front door of his own school. Inscribed on it were the words: "In memory of a once fluid man, crammed and distorted by the classical mess." "That," Lee told *Black Belt* magazine, "expresses my feelings perfectly."

There is evidence, however, that Lee was not as hysterically opposed to the classical arts as he liked people to think. He undoubtedly owed much of his own discipline and ability to classical training, and it would be unlike him to forget that. His love of playing devil's advocate in the stuffy, confined atmosphere of the ancient Martial Arts chambers led him to berate and exaggerate, to attempt to inject some life and necessary change into his "first love" - the Martial Arts: "By Martial Art, I mean an unrestricted athletic expression of an individual soul. Martial Art also means daily hermit-like physical training to upgrade or maintain one's quality. To live is to express oneself freely in creation. Creation, I must say, is not a fixed something or a solidification. So I hope my fellow Martial Artists will open up and be transparently real and I wish them well in their own process of finding their cause."

Whether, after so many insults and such terrible tirades, Lee really thought that they would take notice of him is difficult to say. But he had faith in Martial Artists as human beings first. He felt that if he respected the humanity of others, they would respect him.

Lee managed still to believe in the liberating force of physical achievement and expressed the idea that like any art, the Martial Arts are ultimately self-knowledge. A punch or kick knocks the hell out of your ego, your fear, or whatever hang-up you have, and leaves you open to express yourself freely.

If Lee had a hobby-horse, this was it. Freedom of expression, of the type which he knew that the old forms could not provide, had stopped providing centuries ago, and which led him to create his own, unique style. There was, in Bruce Lee's book, no use for partition, or useless structure: "Now the unfortunate thing is," he told a Hong Kong interviewer, bringing the problem back home, "there's Boxing, which uses hands, and judo, which is throwing. I'm not putting them down, mind you, but I am saying that this is a bad thing, because of styles, people are separated. They are not united together because styles become law, man.

"The original founder of the style started out with hypotheses. But now it has become the gospel truth, and people who go into that become the product of it. It doesn't matter who you are, how you are, how you are structured, how you are built, how you are made - it doesn't seem to matter. You just go in there and become that product.

"And to me, that's not right."

THE WISDOM OF BRUCE LEE

CHAPTER THREE

NOT ONE, BUT ALL
Jeet Kune Do is Born

"The wise soldier knows how to marshal the ranks where there are no ranks, can bare the arms to fight where there are no arms to bare, advances against the enemy where there is no enemy. Thus it is that when opposing weapons are crossed, he who deplores the situation conquers."

- LAO TZU

NOT ONE, BUT ALL
Jeet Kune Do is Born

"The wise soldier knows how to marshal the ranks where there are no ranks, can bare the arms to fight where there are no arms to bare, advances against the enemy where there is no enemy. hus it is that when opposing weapons are crossed, he who deplores the situation conquers."

- LAO TZU

Bruce Lee, as an exceptionally talented Martial Artist, and an equally effective self-publicist, was quick to get his own style of Kung Fu accepted as a valid style. As a consequence of this, he was invited onto Hong Kong television in the company of several other, more classical, masters. Each of them discussed and promoted his own style for several minutes.

Then one of the older men stood up under the bright lights, took a fighting stance, and invited each of his co-participants to push him over. One by one, they tried and failed.

Only Lee remained, and the older man jeered at him, taunting him to come over and try to push him out of his stance. Lee got to his feet and walked slowly over. He looked the man up and down, and punched him hard in the face, knocking him out of his stance and flat onto his back.

There was uproar in the studio. An outraged classical master seized Lee by the arm and demanded to know why he'd done such a thing. Lee shrugged. "I don't push," he said. "I punch."

A friend of Lee's, Adrian Marshall, tells the following story about sparring with him: "Bruce tied me up like a pretzel so that I couldn't move. I stood there, totally frustrated -whatever I tried, Bruce could counter it with ease. 'Try something else,' commanded Bruce. 'What?' I shouted angrily. 'What can I do?' 'You could always bite,' laughed Bruce. But he meant it. In one of his films, the villain ties him up in a wrestling hold. So what does he do? He bites!"

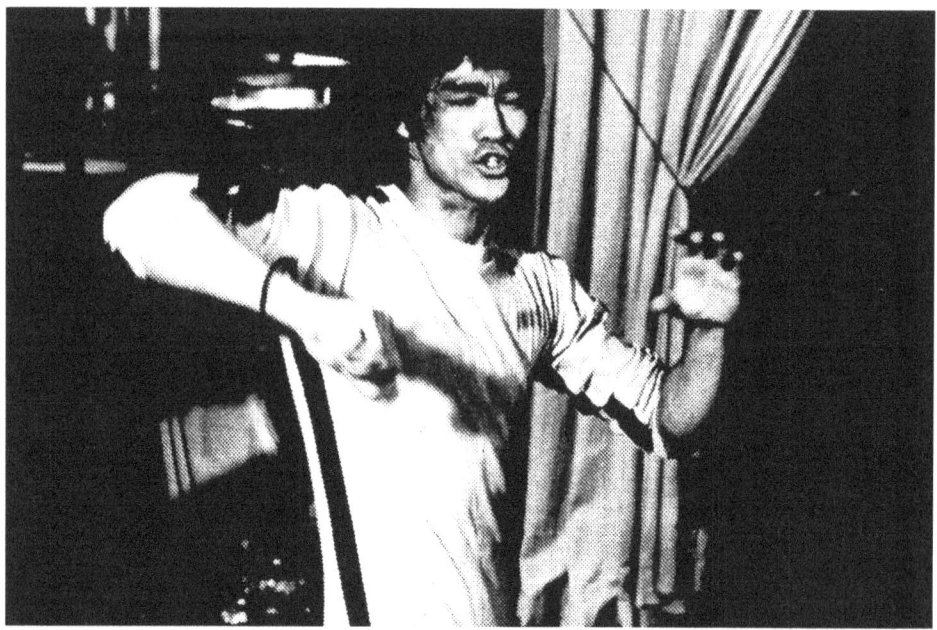

These two tales speak volumes about Bruce Lee's philosophy of the Martial Arts, and about the style which he named Jeet Kune Do. Jeet Kune Do was a style that was not a style, a discipline that owed everything to the classical styles, and owed them nothing. Jeet Kune Do, in Lee's mind, was about directness and about winning fights by any means necessary.

Lee explained: "In building a statue, a sculptor doesn't keep adding clay to his subject. Actually, he keeps chiselling away at the inessentials until the truth is revealed without obstructions. Jeet Kune Do doesn't mean adding more. It means to minimise. In other words, to back away the inessentials. It is not a 'daily increase' but a 'daily decrease.' Art is really the expression of the self. The more complicated and restricted the method, the less the opportunity for the expression of one's original sense of freedom. Though they play an important role in the early stage, the techniques should not be too mechanical, complex or restrictive. If we blindly cling to them, we will eventually become bound by their limitations. Remember, you are expressing the techniques and not doing the techniques. If somebody attacks you, your response is not Technique No. 1, Stance No. 2, Section 4, Paragraph 5. Instead, you simply move in like sound and echo, without any deliberation."

The name Jeet Kune Do must be broken down for understanding. Jeet means to stalk, to intercept. Kune means both style, and fist. And Do means the only way, the reality. Translated into linear Western thinking, the phrase means that the ultimate purpose is to find your opponent, reach him, and strike. It is an offensive, rather than defensive, stratagem. Lee once described it as, "A sophisticated form of street-fighting," which was a natural enough way of looking at the Martial Arts for a youth with his brutal groundwork in the street-gangs of Hong Kong.

He seemed first to begin moving towards a definition of Jeet Kune Do in the early sixties, when he started his own Martial Arts institute on University Way, Seattle. His first prospectus makes interesting reading. The techniques taught at his institute were, he promised, "Smooth, short, and extremely fast; they are direct, to the point and are stripped down to their essential purpose without any wasted motions."

And the difference between Lee's institute and others that the potential Martial Artist might encounter? In the spelling and grammar of a young Easterner with too few months in the West behind him, Lee explained: "Most systems of Martial Art accumulate fancy mess that distort and cramp their pratitioners (sic) and distract them from the actual reality of combat, which is simple and direct. Instead of going immediately to the heart of things, flowery forms and artificial techniques are ritually presented to simulate actual combat. Thus instead of being in combat these pratitioners are 'doing' something 'about' combat. Worse still, super mental power and spiritual this and spiritual that are desperately incorporated until these pratitioners are drifting further and further into the distance of mystery and abstraction that what they do resembles anything from acrobatics to modern dancing but the actual reality of combat."

Fortunately for Lee, his grasp of grammar and spelling increased at a commensurate rate with his alienation from "flowery forms," "artificial techniques," and their various "pratitioners."

As the keynote of Jeet Kune Do was simplicity, the stripping down of the sculpture to bare necessities, it became necessary to deny that he had actually "invented" a new "style" - to argue, in fact," that the word "style" was pointless and irrelevant.

"Fundamentally," he explained, "all styles claim their methods are able to cope with all types of attack. That means each and every style is complete and total; in other words their structure covers all possible lines and angles as well as being capable of retaliating from all angles and lines. Since all possible lines and angles are covered, whence come all these 'different' styles?"

Lee posed the question and emphasised his irony by saying that a man who claims his style is really different must stand on his head when he strikes, and turn and spin three times before doing so. There just aren't that many ways to come in on an opponent without deviating from the natural and direct path. Different instructors may go only for straight lines, or maybe round lines, or maybe only kicking, or maybe even just looking different, but styles that cling to one partial aspect of combat are actually in bondage. Actual combat is never fixed, and Lee felt that formalised resistance hampered you in actual combat.

And more succinctly, he informed the readers of *Black Belt* magazine in 1971: "Let it be understood once and for all that I have not invented a new style, composite, or modification. I have in no way set Jeet Kune Do within a distinct form governed by laws that distinguish it from 'this' style or 'that' method. On the contrary, I hope to free my comrades from bondage to styles, patterns, and doctrines."

So what, asked many critics, was so special about Jeet Kune Do, so urgent and original? Well, answered Lee, I am offering you a universal style, a Martial Arts philosophy which ignores racial barriers and will consequently bring together fighters who were previously separated by unnecessary geographical differences. He explained:

"Many people who come to instruction would say, like, 'Hey, man, like what is the truth? Hand it over to me.' So therefore one guy would say, 'I'll give you my Japanese way of doing it. In Jeet Kune Do, nationalities don't mean anything. I mean, at least you can say there are different approaches. We must approach it as an expression of ourself. When you go to a Japanese style, then you are expressing a Japanese style. You are not expressing yourself."

But "universality" alone would be meaningless. What of the brash new "directness" that Lee claimed to offer. A reporter from *Black Belt* asked Lee what this "directness" was all about?

Hardly had the question left his lips when Lee's wallet came flying through the air at him. He caught it, and Lee laughed.

"That," he said, "is directness. You did what comes naturally. You didn't waste time. You just reached up and caught the wallet and you didn't squat, grunt or go into a horse stance or embark on some such classical move before reaching out for the wallet. You wouldn't have caught it if you had."

And this so-called "simplicity," exactly what did that mean? Lee borrowed a Zen truism to illustrate his point: "Before I studied the art, a punch to me was just like a punch, a kick just like a kick. After I'd first learned the art, a punch was no longer a punch, a kick no longer a kick. Now that I've understood the art, a punch is just like a punch, a kick just like a kick.

"The height of cultivation is nothing special. It is merely simplicity, the ability to express the utmost with the minimum. It is the halfway cultivation that leads to ornamentation."

Jeet Kune Do, concluded Lee, was, "basically a sophisticated fighting style stripped to its essentials." And he mockingly added: "The disciples are very proud to be accepted in this exclusive style."

To those who looked to Jeet Kune Do for "extraordinary" powers, Lee had disappointing words. His version of the Martial Arts was about the purely earthly business of developing one's natural talents and abilities: "Don't disregard your five natural senses in the search for a so-called sixth," he said. "Just develop your five natural senses."

Similarly, the mystical system of "rankings" in the Martial Arts was abruptly turned inside out by a ruthless Lee: "We do have a unique ranking system in our particular style," he admitted. "Actually, I should say a ranking system of no ranking. The first rank is a blank circle, which signifies original freedom. The second rank is green and white in the form of the yin/yang symbol with two curved arrows around it. The third is purple and white, the fourth is grey and white, the fifth is red and white, the sixth is gold and white, the seventh is red and gold, which is our school's emblem; and the eighth rank is the highest, which is a blank circle, the return to the beginning stage. "In other words, all the previous rank certificates are useful for cleaning up messes."

"There is no rule that has been set down," said Lee at another time, and it could well stand as his epitaph in the world of the Martial Arts, "that cannot be broken. It might have been functional at one time, but it may not be functional today."

In some ways, though, Jeet Kune Do conformed to the strictest of ancient Martial Arts codes in its eschewal of weaponry, for instance. The great philosopher/poet, Lao Tzu, wrote many centuries ago that: "Weapons, however beautiful, are instruments of evil omen, hateful, it may be said, to all creatures. These sharp instruments are not the tools of the superior man - he uses them solely on the compulsion of necessity. Calm and repose are his true weapons, while victory by force of arms a painful resort. To consider weapons desirable would be to delight in the slaughter of men; and he who delights in the slaughter of men cannot get his true will on earth. He who has killed multitudes of men should weep for them with the bitterest of grief."

Lee's attitudes toward "sharp instruments" more or less coincided with Lao Tzu's. He many times expressed regret for the profligacy of his switchblade, street-gang youth; and while he claimed for Jeet Kune Do the mantle of "most effective, expedient style," the expediency stopped comfortably short of the use of artificial aids. Lee wanted his body to be able to do all the work, unassisted.

The one obvious exception to all of this is, of course, the nunchakus. Lee used nunchaku sticks (two short hard teak blackjacks connected by about two feet of chain, to be swung like bolas or whipped like a mace) on film several times, and had obviously mastered well the tricky business of fighting with them. We can, however, be sure of one thing: Lee did not learn that art by practicing on a human being, and he never introduced his Jeet Kune Do students to the nunchakus.

Rather, he recognised the cinematic appeal of the sticks, the thrill of their viciously carved parabolas through the air, in the hands of a master such as Lee. Essentially, Lee thought that any Martial Artist worth his salt should be easily capable of withstanding a

nunchaku attack barehanded. In the words of Chuang Tzu: "Men who work on the waters do not shrink from meeting sharks and whales - that is the courage of the fisherman. Men who work on the land do not shrink from meeting tigers and rhinoceroses - that is the courage of the hunter. When men see sharp weapons crossed before them and look on death as going home - that is the courage of the determined warrior."

For a time, it seemed as though Lee would break the cardinal rule of the Martial Arts: by refusing to open his own school when given the opportunity of ready cash by businessmen charmed by his *Green Hornet* appearances. He said:

"I was approached by several businessmen to open a franchise for Kato's Self-defence School, but I refused." And although he had written a book called *Tao of Jeet Kune Do*, he never allowed it to be published. "I felt then, as I still feel today," he said in 1973, "that I am not going to prostitute the art for the sake of money." Lee also realised that others were not to be trusted: "That's why I didn't publish the book - some guys would read it, and then open schools using my name as their instructor."

So, since his death, our knowledge of the concepts behind Jeet Kune Do are limited. The basics are apparent, they were laid down by Lee with sufficient clarity. But for the finer points, even for some of the practical applications, we are left to piece together the whole picture from snippets of information that he left us. Some of these remnants are invaluable guides to the nature of Jeet Kune Do. This letter to fellow Martial Artist Danny Inosanto is one such guide: "The International Karate Championship uses my three stages of cultivation of Kung Fu in its international Karate emblem. The first stage is the primitive stage. It is a stage of original ignorance in which a person knows nothing about the art of combat. In a fight, he simply blocks and strikes instinctively without a concern for what is right and wrong. Of course, he may not be so-called scientific, but, nevertheless, being himself, his attacks or defences are fluid.

"The second stage - the stage of sophistication, or mechanical stage - begins when a person starts his training. He is taught the different ways of blocking, striking, kicking, standing, breathing, and thinking. Unquestionably, he has gained the scientific knowledge of combat, but unfortunately his original self and sense of freedom are lost, and his action no longer flows by itself. His mind tends to freeze at different movements for calculations and analysis, and, even worse, he might be called 'intellectually bound' and maintain himself outside the actual reality.

"The third stage - the stage of alertness, or spontaneous stage - occurs when, after years of serious and hard practice, he realises that after all, Kung Fu is nothing special. And instead of trying to impose on his mind, he adjusts himself to his opponent like water pressing on an earthen wall. It flows through the slightest crack. There is nothing to do but try to be purposeless and formless, like water. All of his classical techniques and standard styles are minimised, if not wiped out, and nothingness prevails. He is no longer confined.

"Dan, forget about fancy horses, about moving the horse, fancy forms, pressure, locking, etc. All these will promote your mechanical aspects rather than help you. You will be bound by these unnatural rhythmic messes, and when you are in combat it is broken rhythm and timing you have to adjust to. The opponent is not going to do things rhythmically with you as you would do in practicing a Kata alone or with a partner."

Later Lee once sighed, "It is indeed difficult to convey simplicity." For people who seemed incapable of appreciating the basic sense and very ordinary truth behind his plea for a return to practicality, he would resort to anecdote and fable: "Two Orientals were watching the Olympic Games in Rome. One of the chief attractions was Bob Hayes, the sprinter, in the hundred-yard run. As the gun went off to set the race in motion, the spectators leaned forward in their seats, tense with excitement. With the runners reaching

their goal, Hayes forged ahead and flashed across the line, the winner with a new world's record of 9.1 seconds.

"As the crowd cheered, one of the Orientals elbowed the other in the ribs and said: 'Did you see that? His heel was too high up!'"

But, while it might be frustrating to be left with such tempting fragments of the Jeet Kune Do philosophy, it is also as Lee would have had it. He had reasons for not sanctifying his "style." He realised that the creation of a huge following would ultimately be self-defeating. As he himself wrote: "It is conceivable that a long time ago a certain Martial Artist discovered some partial truth. During his lifetime, the man resisted the temptation to organize this partial truth, although this is a common tendency in man's search for security and certainty in life.

"After his death, his students took 'his' hypothesis, 'his' postulates, 'his' inclination, and 'his' method and turned them into law. Impressive creeds were then invented, solemn reinforcing ceremonies prescribed, rigid philosophy and patterns formulated, and so on, until finally an institution was erected.

"So, what originated as one man's intuition of some sort of personal fluidity has been transformed into solidified, fixed knowledge, complete with organized classified responses presented in a logical order. In so doing, the well-meaning, loyal followers have not only made this knowledge a holy shrine, but also a tomb in which they have buried the founder's wisdom."

Undeterred, interviewers and curious friends would constantly attempt to pull Lee into putting his stamp of approval onto one particular style or form of the Martial Arts. There must be some preference, suggested one interviewer shortly before his death, one style which was, by itself, more effective than the others. Karate? Judo? Chinese Boxing? Which would it be?

"There is," Lee patiently explained, "no such thing as an effective segment of a totality. By that I mean that I do not personally believe in the word 'style.' Why? Because, unless there are human beings with three arms and four legs, unless we have another group of beings on earth which are structurally different from us, there can be no different style of fighting.

"Why is that? Because we have two hands and two legs. The important thing is: how can we use them to the maximum effect."

So, the guidelines that Lee laid for those who wished to follow the non-doctrine of Jeet Kune Do were as clear as they needed to be, which is to say, necessarily obscure:

"You must accept the fact," he wrote, "that there is no help but self-help. For the same reason, I cannot tell you how to 'gain' freedom, since freedom exists within you. I cannot tell you how to 'gain' self-knowledge. While I can tell you what not to do, I cannot tell you what you should do, since that would be confining you to a particular approach. Formulas can only inhibit freedom, externally dictated prescriptions only squelch creativity and assure mediocrity.

"Bear in mind that the freedom that accrues from self-knowledge cannot be acquired through strict adherence to a formula; we do not suddenly 'become' free, we simply 'are' free.

"Abide by the principle," said Bruce Lee to Danny Inosanto. "Dissolve the principle, obey the principle without being bound to it - Jeet Kune Do!"

THE KUNG-FU MONTHLY ARCHIVE SERIES

CHAPTER FOUR

A FINGER POINTING AT THE MOON
On Training and Keeping Fit

"Strength by itself is not equal to knowledge, and knowledge is not equal to training; but combine knowledge with training, and one will get strength."

— ANONYMOUS

A FINGER POINTING AT THE MOON
On Training and Keeping Fit

"Strength by itself is not equal to knowledge, and knowledge is not equal to training; but combine knowledge with training, and one will get strength."

- ANONYMOUS

Of all his many assets, Bruce Lee valued his body most. He went to lengths that many regarded as eccentric, even fanatical, to keep his physique in perfect shape. His gymnasium was a temple to physical fitness, equipped with every kind of apparatus and lined with mirrors, that the athlete might better observe his own exercises and contortions.

There were aspects of his campaign to maintain perfect health which were not recommendable to others. For instance, while he rightly took great care about what he ingested into his system, believing that "you are what you eat," and consequently eschewed tobacco or alcohol; Lee's diet frequently left much to be desired. For a period, he seemed to subsist almost entirely on vitamin pills, at another time he ate nothing but steak (rare), and drank cow's blood. Robert, his brother, describes arriving in America and being met at the airport by Bruce, who stepped back with a horrified expression, and exclaimed: "Jesus, you're skinny! Don't tell anyone you're my brother - you'll embarrass me."

The younger Lee was then rushed to his brother's home in Bel Air. Next morning he was wakened early, handed a pair of tennis shoes, and made to run three miles. Soon, Bruce had also devised a suitable diet for Robert, who was not altogether grateful: "Boy, that was really a torture. Bruce was like a drill sergeant. He'd mix it everyday himself to make sure I'd drink it. It had milk, quick-weight-gain protein powder, banana, ice-cream, egg-shells and peanut butter. He made me drink a quart every day."

The essence of physical fitness, the spring-board from which all novices must move to a state of readiness to study the Martial Arts, is perfection of breathing. And however simple that might sound, the art of breathing is actually a complex, much abused one. Basically, most people (including Lee, probably, before Ip Man took him in hand and showed his young pupil the better way) breathe in too shallow a manner. Most of us breathe from the chest. We ought to breathe from the belly.

The advantage of using the diaphragm rather than the torso when inhaling and exhaling air is simply that the former method empties the lungs and fills them more efficiently and thoroughly. The practical medical benefits of this are obvious. But the effects of the exercise on the beginner go much further. By breathing in deeply through the nose and exhaling through the mouth, taking care all the while that the chest remains still and unexerted and the stomach does the work, the Martial Artist increases his stock of chi- with all of the advantages of powerful inner calm that that implies.

The remarkable John F. Gilbey relates a story told to him by another maestro of the Martial Arts, Donn Draeger, which indicates that the power of training the breath has unusual possibilities - possibilities that Bruce Lee most certainly never mastered!

Draeger met in France in the early 1950s a man named Henri Pougard, and they took to discussing the importance of breathing exercises in the Martial Arts. Pougard simply said that he considered it possible to lay too much emphasis on their importance, but he had developed a fighting art in which his own breath, disciplined and controlled, became an offensive weapon. He had developed the Halitotic Attack. He had developed its powers by practicing on stray animals, and was now capable of breathing on a human

such vile odors as to make him or her faint clean away.

Obviously fascinated, Draeger asked Pougard for a demonstration, with himself as vic-tim. His account is memorable: "From across his dining room table - a distance of about six feet - he breathed on me.

"I watched him, my senses acute. I thought, what a big mouth when opened wide; almost like Joe E. Brown. Then the odour, smell, no - stink - hit me. A garbage dump, ren- dering plant, tannery-this beat them all. Of course I didn't have time to analyze it then. For the onslaught of that stink was like a physical strike. I gasped for breath that wasn't there, gasped again with the same result, and fainted. "I woke to Henri's laughing ban- ter." Perhaps, on consideration, it is as well that there were some strikes that Bruce Lee left unmastered.

But Bruce Lee will not be remembered as a dietician, nor should he be. His body was developed into a model of muscular grace, avoiding both the overdone lumpen clumsiness of the weightlifter or Mr. Body Beautiful contestant, and the unattractively Spartan sinews of the long-distance runner. Lee's body was an instrument of genuine beauty, and he got it that way through a series of carefully designed exercises and workouts which, fortunately, have been recorded and left to us in a plethora of interviews, articles, and private reminiscences. The development of such a physique, however, as Lee was eager to point out, is not an end in itself. It is rather, he said: "A finger pointing at the moon. Please do not take the finger to be the moon, or fix your gaze so intently on the finger as

to miss the beautiful sights of heaven. After all, the usefulness of the finger is in pointing away from itself to the light which illumines finger and all."

The best way of maintaining a constant level of physical excellence, and of establishing a base of fitness from which one might progress, was according to Lee the humble art of jogging. Throughout his life, he recommended this easily available exercise to anybody interested, saying: "If you are not physically fit, you have no business doing any hard sparring. To me, the best exercise for this is running. Running is so important that you should keep it up during your lifetime. What time of the day you run is not important as long as you run. In the beginning you should jog easily, then gradually increase the distance and tempo, and finally include sprinting to develop your wind."

Lee himself ran six days a week, for between fifteen and forty-five minutes (two to six miles) a day, usually in the enthusiastic company of his pet Great Dane, Bobo.

Another form of regular exercise that Lee employed was Tai Chi. Shortly after dawn in most oriental cities, the traveler will observe scores of men, from the very young to the very old, performing a series of slow-motion twists and contortions. These are Tai Chi exercises. Their advantage is that, like jogging, you don't need a gymnasium to practice Tai Chi. The exercises can be done on a sidewalk, in an office, or in a public park. They are therapy for the mind as well as the body, meditation as well as physical exercise.

The story of the origin of Tai Chi comes from a monk named Chang San-feng. Chang was meditating one noon, when a noise interrupted his concentration, and caused him

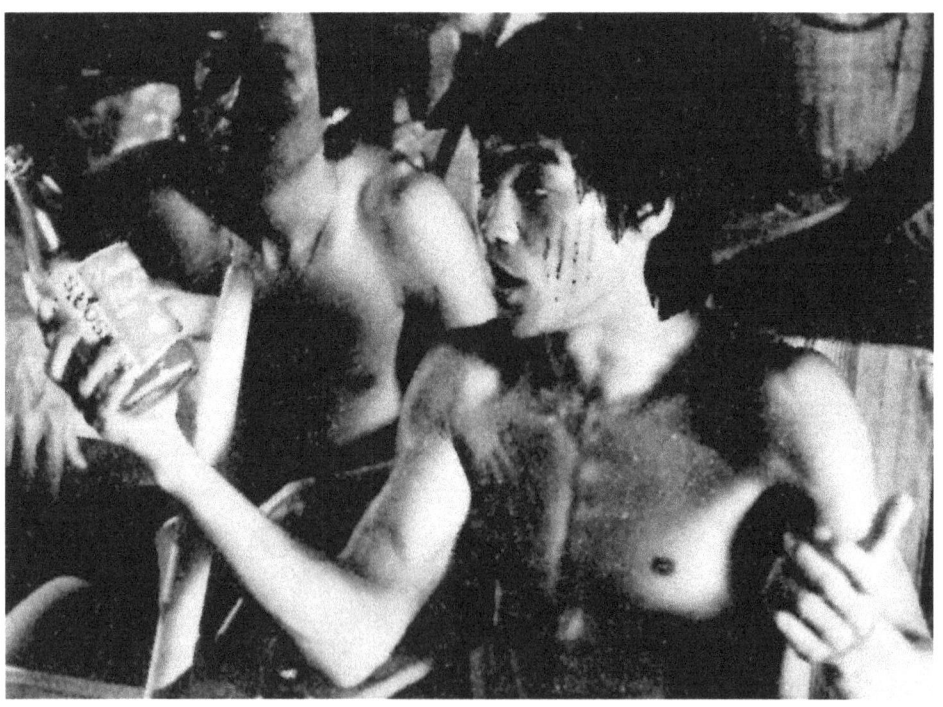

to look outside. There was a snake, head erect and spitting, under attack from a crane. As the crane swooped down, the snake swerved to one side, striking the crane with its tail as the bird flew past. If the crane protected one part of its body in an attack, the snake was able to swerve and glide into position to strike another, always out of reach, leaving the crane an impotent and disillusioned aggressor. Finally, the crane gave up, and flew away frustrated. The snake slithered back into its hole.

Chang then saw the value of the weak bending under attack from the strong: the concept of the I Ching. So he began to study such methods of combat used by animals, and prepared them into the style of exercise known as Tai Chi; based on the principle: "What is more yielding than water? Yet back it comes to wear down the stone."

Lee himself, speaking of such exercises, once told a reporter: "Like water, it should be formless. Pour it into a cup, it becomes part of the cup. Pour it into a bottle, it becomes part of the bottle. Try to kick or punch it, it is resilient. Clutch it, and it will yield without hesitation. In fact, it will escape as pressure is being applied to it. How true it is that nothingness cannot be confined. The softest thing cannot be snapped."

Bruce Lee never really rested from such exercises. Friends would say that they never saw him at leisure, even while chatting over dinner or watching television, he would be pressing his palm against the underside of the table, or flexing his thigh muscles. Linda describes how she would frequently find him with a book in one hand and a dumb-bell in the other, and how he would jump up from the most intriguing conversation to jot down a new exercise that had just crossed his mind. James Coburn tells a story about flying with Lee, when Lee would alternately pound a writing pad with either fist. After a while the irritated Coburn complained.

"Sorry man," apologised Lee. "I've got to keep in shape."

Of all "natural" exercises - that is, exercises that require no special equipment or are geared to no special technique-that Lee employed, probably the most useful were his iso-metric exercises. An isometric exercise is simply one whereby the muscles are improved by pitting them against an immovable object- such as a wall. Lee would stand for an hour or more pushing the backs of his hands up against his balcony railings.

To prove to yourself how much tension this can inject into your arm muscles, try standing close to a wall, facing it. Now, standing perfectly upright, push hard against the wall with the back of your hands, and keep pushing for three or four minutes. Take a step back from the wall, letting your arms hang loose, and they will rise of their own free will several inches into the air. Now try doing it for an hour or more.

Lee used isometric exercises to develop most of the muscles in his body. As a particularly effective way of putting stress on as many muscles as possible with the one exercise, it would be difficult to better the "isometric bar" that he improvised in his gym. This was a metal bar, heavily padded about the middle, which could be slotted at any height in between two vertical pieces of scaffolding. When it was slotted so, usually at just under shoulder height, Lee would stoop under it, rest his shoulders and the back of his neck up against the padding, and push up. Thus calf, thigh, and stomach muscles could be exercised. And by placing his hands on either side of the padding, and pushing up with them too, the arm muscles could be brought into play.

Lee referred to his hands and feet, his arms and legs, as "the tools of the trade," and would consequently go to any lengths to keep them honed into workman-like shape. But of the exercises that he used, he insisted: "A drill has to be functional. It has to be close to reality."

Lee's kicking was so functional that the Chinese nicknamed him "the man with three legs." Lee developed this fast, high kick through careful use of the gym cycle, and leg stretches onto a high bar. When the muscles were developed, and ready, he would start kicking trees. Yes, trees and not puny "saplings, but full-grown palm trees. "When you can kick," he said, "so you aren't jarred, but the tree is jarred, then you will begin to understand a kick."

Another unlikely victim of his kicking abilities was the two-hundred-pound heavy bag, not normally used for such ends: "I like to swing the heavy bag, and if I can stop it with a kick, I know I can knock a four-hundred-pound man on his ass."

In practicing backward hook-kicks, he would stand a colleague up against the back of a heavy bag, while Lee kicked it. The colleague would more often than not be thrown across the room, and certainly jolted off his feet.

But none of these workouts could compensate for what Lee called the "secret" of kicking - commitment to the blow. Danny Inosanto remembers Lee passing on a confidential piece of advice: "The secret of kicking, as Bruce taught it, was controlled anger. I remember once he asked me to try kicking. He held this shield and for five minutes I kicked at that shield desperately trying to improve my kick. I really thought I was giving my all but Bruce still wasn't satisfied. Finally, he came over and slapped me on the face, at the same time calling out, 'Now, kick!' He held up the shield. I was simply blazing with anger and went POW! It was fantastic."

To develop his punch, Lee mainly used various kinds of bags. He preferred the older type of punching speed bag (which is supported by a pair of sprung cords) to the more modern "platform" speed bag, because: "It teaches you to hit straight and square. If you don't hit it straight, the bag will not return directly to you. Besides teaching footwork, you can hit the bag upward, too. Another important function is that after the delivery of the punch the bag will return instantaneously, which teaches you to be alert and to recover quickly."

The rules of working out with a heavy bag, according to Lee, were that the fighter should always keep himself covered, and never leave gaps in his defence while sparring with the bag, which he should "fight as if it is your opponent." Footwork should be used, of every different type-side-steps, feints, etc., and the type of blow delivered to the bag should also vary.

The bag should not be treated lightly or delicately; it should not be daintily pawed at, but the fighter should rather: "Explode through it, and remember that the power of the kick and punch comes from the correct contact at the right spot and at the right moment with the body in perfect position" and not from mere brute power or thoughtless force.

Lee used a round punching bag to perfect punches to the face, and a "jabbing pad" to develop speed and power of jabs at the eyes. A paper target, being simply a sheet of paper hanging on a rope, helps develop a sense of the proper application of power against a given object. Lee's jabs increased the speed and accuracy of his hands and fingers to phenomenal degrees. A friend, Adrian Marshall, describes the following example of sleight of hand that a magician would envy: "Bruce put this dime in my hand and then said, 'Let's see how fast you are - when I reach out for that dime, you close your fist and see if you can stop me from getting it.' Well, he moved once, and I closed my fist, and then he moved again, and once again I got my fist shut before he could grab the dime.

"The third time everything seemed to move a bit faster, but when I closed my fist, I still had that dime tightly clutched. Or at least I thought I had! When I opened my fist, not only had the dime gone but there was a penny lying in my hand instead."

THE WISDOM OF BRUCE LEE

Other friends remember similar tricks through which Lee would demonstrate his astonishing reflex speed, such as throwing a punch so fast that they couldn't see it, but so close to the face that the recipient could feel a draught; or asking a friend to hold his hand up by his chin, and then try to stop Lee closing his (the friend's) eyelids. Inevitably, Lee was able to close his victim's eyelids so quickly that his hand was away before it could be intercepted, and so tenderly that the "guinea-pig" hardly felt it. Such was the payoff of intensive training.

The power of Lee's hands and fingers were as awesome as their speed and accuracy. An understanding of just one exercise that he used to improve this power should be

enough: Lee could do one-finger push-ups. It is obviously pointless to demand of aspiring Martial Artists that they follow the master into this particular area - try it and see why!

And even if you succeed, Lee had more in store: "Remember," he said, "just because you get very good at this supplemental training, it should not go to your head that you're an expert. Remember, actual sparring is the ultimate, and this training is only a means toward it."

In order to prepare himself more thoroughly for sparring, and obeying his own dictum that "everything must be functional," Lee had a special dummy constructed, which he trans-ported from Hong Kong to the States. It was six feet tall and twelve inches in diameter. It had two "arms" just below the "neck," and another at about waist-height, all three stretching out two feet, as well as a metal "leg" stretching out and down at the base. This swung round when Lee hit the arms higher up the dummy, and thus taught him to use his own leg to block an opponent's kick.

About sparring itself, Lee had revolutionary ideas. He did not believe in always sparring with those of distinct martial style, nor in pulling punches: "In sparring," he said, "you should wear suitable protective equipment and go all out. Then you can truly learn the correct timing and distance for the delivery of kicks, punches, etc. It's a good idea to spar with all kinds of individuals - tall, short, fast, clumsy - yes, at times a clumsy fellow will mess up a better man because his awkwardness serves as a sort of broken rhythm.

"The best sparring partner, though, is a quick strong man who does not know anything, a mad man who goes all-out, scratching, grabbing, punching, kicking, etc." This variety of sparring experience would, Lee was sure, equip a fighter to handle any kind of opponent - Boxer, Judoka, Wrestler, or any other kind. Lee would tell Danny Inosanto in sparring: "Come in like a Boxer would come in. Come in swinging like a street fighter would swing."

This training pattern was an intrinsic part of the Jeet Kune Do philosophy. If other styles could cope so well with "every kind of attack," then why, he asked provocatively, are there so many different styles? Training should not be a routine, a set drill, it should alter with mood and necessity. The fighter, claimed Lee, "should be alive in sparring, throwing punches and kicks from all angles, not a cooperative robot." And Lee's old dedication to "efficiency" manifested here more than anywhere. "Efficiency" in sparring was "anything that scores," he spurned "fancy forms and classical sets."

"For something," he said, "that is static, fixed, dead, there can be a way or a definite path, but not to anything that is moving and living. In sparring, there's no exact path or method but, instead, a perceptive, pliable, choiceless awareness. It lives from moment to moment.

"The idea of hard versus soft and internal versus external is not important. The yin and yang is in reality two halves of a whole. Each half is equally important and each is interdependent on the other. If one rejects either the firm or the gentle, this will lead to one extreme. Those who cling to either extreme are known as the physical-bound or the intellectual-bound. But the former are more bearable, at least in combat they do struggle."

Lee's training methods are not easy to present as a textbook on "How to Keep Fit," because apart from the fact that his methods were geared to the physical standards of his own body, which was an extraordinary one, they also were constantly changing to suit Lee's needs of the moment. He would never tolerate a drill just for its own sake, and had little time for ineffectual exercises: "Dan," he told Inosanto, "if it doesn't work for you, throw it away. But you should drill on it first."

If a drill had limited purpose, however, he would find a way of adapting it to his needs, saying, "Turn the stumbling block into a step-ping stone." As when he injured his back in a car crash in Oakland, and his friends feared for his fighting ability. Lee adapted a "gravity" instrument so that he could hang upside down by the legs, stretching and exercising.

"How can I be so well co-ordinated?" he once asked himself. "Well, I have to be an athlete using jogging and all those basic ingredients. Right, and after all that you ask yourself, how can you honestly express yourself at that moment? And being yourself, when you punch, you really want to punch - not trying to punch because you're trying to avoid getting hit, but to really be in with it and express yourself.

"The most important thing to me is, how in the process of learning how to use my body, can I come to understand myself?"

THE WISDOM OF BRUCE LEE

CHAPTER FIVE

I CAN GIVE
YOU THE TOOLS
The Teacher and the Student

"Although a sword is sharp, without the frequent use of the grindstone, it will not cut. Although a man's natural abilities be excellent, without learning he will not rise high. The spirits may be good and the viands admirable, but until you taste them you do not know their flavour. Principles may be good, but until you learn them you do not know their value. Hence it is by learning that a man knows his deficiencies."

- HAN YING

I CAN GIVE YOU THE TOOLS
The Teacher and the Student

"Although a sword is sharp, without the frequent use of the grindstone, it will not cut. Although a man's natural abilities be excellent, without learning he will not rise high. The spirits may be good and the viands admirable, but until you taste them you do not know their flavour. Principles may be good, but until you learn them you do not know their value. Hence it is by learning that a man knows his deficiencies."

- HAN YING

There is an ancient Zen story that Bruce Lee was fond of telling people who came to him for tuition. It tells of how a learned man once went to a Zen teacher to find out about Zen. The Zen teacher willingly complied, and began explaining. But as his story unfolded, the learned man frequently interrupted with remarks like, "Oh, yes, I know of that already," and "That is of course a part of many philosophies."

Finally, the Zen teacher stopped talking and began to serve tea to the learned man. He filled his guest's cup, and still kept pouring, until the cup overflowed. "Enough," cried the learned man. "My cup is already full."

"Indeed, so I see," replied the Zen master. "And if you do not empty it first, how can you expect to taste my cup of tea?"

"The usefulness of the cup," Lee would point out, "is its emptiness."

He started teaching while still a student at the University of Washington, Seattle. Before that, to support himself, he had "just taken any kind of job around. Like most Chinese kids who had just gotten off the boat, my first job was bussing and washing dishes in a restaurant."

But he soon discovered that there was an eager enough student audience, wanting to tap his knowledge of the Martial Arts, so he opened class in a carpark. At the time, he professed indifference: "I didn't really care about teaching Kung Fu, but it sure beat washing dishes."

It was at one such class that Lee met the attractive, slim, brown-haired girl named Linda who was to become his wife. "Somehow," remembered Linda, "he was able to enchant his audience."

In later days, Lee was to grow wary of trying to teach women the Martial Arts, claiming that they did not have the natural advantages of a man. He explained to the Hong Kong press:

"I advise a female learning Kung Fu that if they are ever attacked, hit 'em in the groin, poke 'em on the shins or the knee and run like hell! Women fighters are all right, but they're no match for the men, who are physiologically stronger except for a few vital points.

"Women are much more likely to achieve their objectives through feminine wiles and persuasion."

At the time, however, Linda Emery was welcome enough - both for her fee and for her pretty face.

Shortly after starting such impromptu classes, Lee left University without qualifying, determined to open his own institute of the Martial Arts. He found a building in University Way, Seattle, and issued his first prospectus (extracts from which are reprinted in "Not Just One, But All Styles," the chapter on Jeet Kune Do). And the man who was later

to charge Hollywood stars such as Steve McQueen several hundred dollars an hour for tuition, offered lessons for twenty-two dollars a month, or seventeen dollars a month for minors.

Although his consuming ambition was to break into movies, Lee found himself becoming gradually more and more fascinated with the philosophies of teaching, with the intricacies of conveying his physical and spiritual message to a variety of pupils. He de-

termined to treat each student differently, as an individual, and not just resort to a set curriculum and standard method of teaching everybody, regardless of personality. This was obviously going to lead to difficulties, at twenty-two dollars a month. Dan Inosanto said of Lee's teaching methods: "He could get you emotionally involved. He didn't like to teach more than three students. In fact, in all his teachings, he never taught more than six students at one time. I think he felt that teaching could not take place if you had more than six students, that you would be drilling like a Karate class, and he didn't want that. He wanted me to carry on the art in the same manner. He said: 'Only have six students, Dan.'"

Lee made it clear that such low numbers were essential if the teacher was to inspire every student to explore himself, "both internally and externally." It was a form of teaching that almost was not teaching at all, he maintained, but was more a question of provoking the student into reaching oneness with himself. He accepted that such teaching was difficult and demanding, but insisted on maintaining it. Only occasionally did he despair, and ruminate on the possibility that his pupils might not be worthy of such effort, as scholars of his own high standards were difficult to come across. Most of his pupils in those early days were "five-minute enthusiasts," some were thugs looking solely for a more efficient way to practice thuggery (a syndrome that Lee understood only too well), and most were simply talentless and without any real imaginative potential. But teaching seemed to suit Bruce Lee, and he persevered.

Ironically, his first major television part was Kung Fu instructor. Lee played the friend of a blind insurance detective, "Longstreet," in the series of the same name. Longstreet demands of Lee that he teach him some martial skills, but Lee becomes frustrated with trying to train the blind man. The exchange which follows between the two, written by one of Lee's actual pupils, Stirling Silliphant, is interesting:

Longstreet: You weren't born being able to take apart three men in a matter of seconds.
Lee: I found the cause of my ignorance.
Longstreet: Well, help me find mine.
Lee: I cannot teach you, I can only help you explore yourself.
Now it is Longstreet's turn to become frustrated, and Lee tells him:
"You have a quarrelsome mind, Mr. Longstreet. Unless you learn to calm it, you will never hear the world outside. You must learn defeat. Like most people, you want to learn to win. To learn to die is to be liberated from it. When tomorrow comes, you must learn to die and be liberated by it."

Lee considered that there were three stages of learning the Martial Arts, and they became the stages around which he based the course at his new school, on new premises in Los Angeles. These stages were:

1) The primitive stage of total ignorance, in which a man or woman knows nothing about the art. Instinct alone prevails in deciding whether to block or attack in combat during this stage.

2) The mechanical, or sophisticated stage, when a pupil has begun his training. In this stage, the pupil has certainly improved in techniques of blocking, striking, kicking, breathing, etc., but there is usually a tendency to lose the instinctive fluidity the pupil possessed in the previous stage. Many Martial Artists, Lee realised, remained in this stage all of their lives, which is why he introduced the revolutionary third stage -

3) Which is that of alertness and spontaneous action. It can only come after years of serious and hard practice, and is the sign of a real master. Without having lost any of the abilities developed in the second stage, the fighter throws his rule book out of the window. That is, he reverts to the fluidity of the untrained man, ready for any combat situation, Karate, boxing, whatever.

The convenient advertising which *Longstreet* and his other part as Kato in *The Green Hornet* gave to Bruce Lee's fighting prowess meant that the clientele at his new Los Angeles school was becoming richer, more celebrated, but not necessarily more capable. He once told the Hong Kong press: "Not every man can take lessons to become a good fighter. He must be a person who is able to relate his training to the circumstances he encounters."

Back in America he stuck to such principles, even when it meant losing large fees and the possibility of valuable introductions. When the forty-nine-year-old Stirling Silliphant (a successful writer and director) finally tracked Lee down after six months spent looking for this talented young Chinese that he'd heard something about, and asked him for lessons, Lee retorted: "No chance. You're far too old."

Silliphant managed to convince Lee that, although he was older than usual for a Martial Arts novice, he was in excellent physical and mental shape, and Lee finally agreed to take him on. Perhaps the great strides made by Silliphant under Lee's tuition led Lee to say once to Danny Inosanto, who had become his chief instructor: "Ability is of no concern. A man's personality is the primary thing, the thing I choose."

By then, Lee's teaching had become a profitable business. On the one hand, he enjoyed teaching Silliphant, McQueen, James Coburn, Elke Sommer, James Garner, Sy Weintraub and others, even though he confessed to being slightly baffled by their enthusiasm:

"It was a very profitable thing to do," he said. "I used to charge five-hundred-dollars for a ten-hour course, and people flocked to the schools. I even doubled the prices and people still kept coming. I had no idea so many people were interested in Chinese boxing."

But on the other hand, he experienced qualms about the dilution of the fighting philosophy which he now knew as Jeet Kune Do in the face of so much glamour and money. He determined not to sell out his art, and instructed Danny Inosanto never to open a commercial school under the name Jeet Kune Do, saying:

"You could probably make some money out of it. But I'd be very disappointed if you did."

Meanwhile, his showbiz pupils found Lee to be an idiosyncratic teacher. He made it clear to them from the very beginning that his was no instant crash course in avoiding sand being kicked in one's face.

"I can give you the tools," he told Coburn, "but you have to develop your own way of

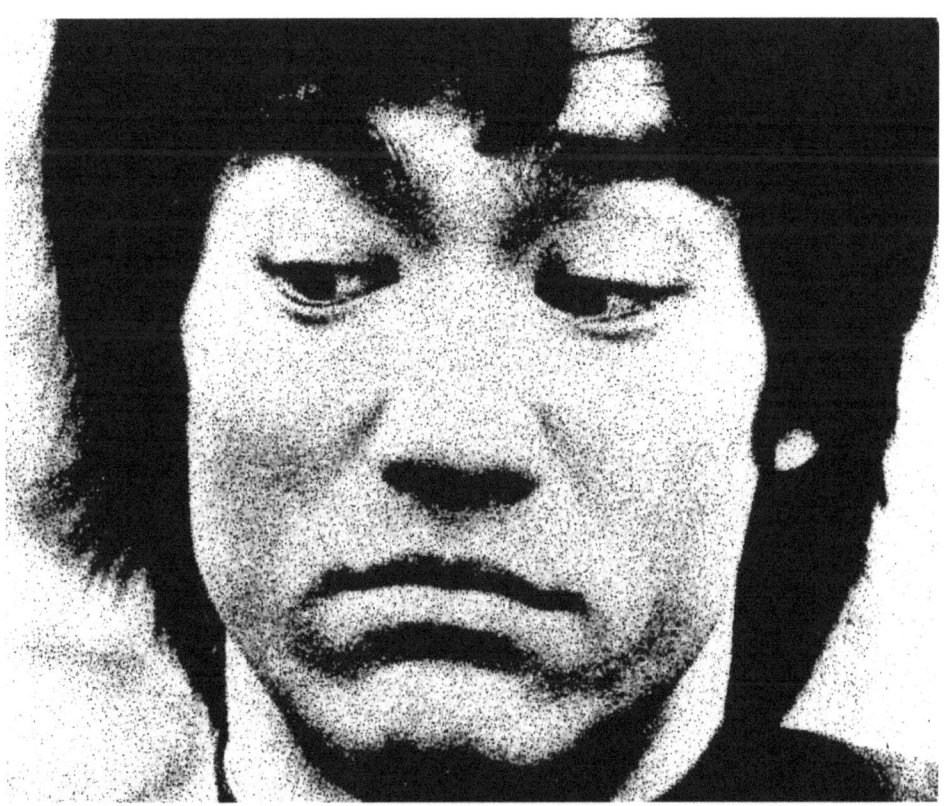

using them." If Coburn looked askance at the aphorism, it was not for long, as Lee handed him a cushion to protect his chest, and demonstrated his famous one-inch punch, knocking Coburn out of a chair and across the room.

Expounding on the "tools" theory, he would add: "Look at any tool as an art. Remember, for a single tool to be a masterpiece, it must have totality, speed, agility, power, flexibility, and accuracy. Until you have the ability to move your body and adapt to whatever the object happens to be in front of you, as well as punch and kick from any angle, you still haven't gotten your total efficiency."

They also found that Lee could be a strict disciplinarian. Once, when a young student found difficulty stretching his leg sufficiently in the kicking exercises, another student giggled mockingly. Lee turned on him ferociously and snapped: "I want you to wipe that smile off your face right this minute or get out of this class."

Two of Lee's celebrity pupils have given accounts of being taught by him which offer fascinating glimpses of the man's methods and personality.

James Coburn describes how Lee took him to one side on his first day and had him run through a few punches, kicks, etc., to assess how far Coburn had developed, and in which direction. Then, for three days a week for the next four or five months, Lee worked solidly with Coburn, and their friendship grew. Coburn admits to being more interested in the esoteric aspects of Kung Fu, while Lee's interest was obviously much wider. Lee would constantly be probing his pupil's abilities, discovering weaknesses and strengths, and pointing to ways of overcoming the former and developing the latter.

"He always had this energy," remembers Coburn. "It was always exploding on him though he channelled it whenever possible, which was most of the time. I mean, he actually created this energy within himself. We'd work out something for an hour and a half and at the end of that time, he'd be filled with force. You really felt high when you'd finished working out with Bruce. He was always trying to bring everything down to one thing - one easy, simple thing."

Coburn describes a workout that Lee called "bridging the gap," which necessitated getting as close to one's opponent as possible to score, without being hit back; and demanded that each party keep a constant eye on the other, which ultimately became a unifying process, drawing the fighters together as one. Lee would let Coburn touch him a couple of times, to give him the idea, and then demonstrate his astonishing speed and mobility.

"But the thing about Bruce that needs to be emphasised as much as anything else was that he himself was constantly learning. I don't think a day went by when he wasn't gathering in some new thing. He'd be bursting with enthusiasm about some new kick he'd just invented - 'Bang! Bang! - look at that, man! Try it, man!' he'd shout, and I'd try it, and the flow of energy was, well, like a whip - always relaxed until right at the end, all the force came out!"

Coburn summarised Lee's mode of instruction as teaching through impressions. "He would lay down an aphorism, a Chinese saying, or a saying that he would have made up out of a combination of Oriental and Western thought, in a way that was applicable to the moment but that could be spread out and be applicable universally. I believe that the Martial Arts are limited and you can only extend them so far, and I believe this is what Bruce found - that there is an absolute limit that you can reach."

THE WISDOM OF BRUCE LEE

There were those, however, who disagreed with Coburn's analysis of Lee's tutorial powers. Ed Parker, for example, considered that Lee's own superlative powers obstructed his understanding of what other, lesser mortals might be capable of achieving.

"He was one in two billion," explained Parker. "If God could give a man all the natural talents, he had them. He was limited by his own philosophy, though. He used to use an analogy about a sculptor, how he has to chip away the inessentials to find the essential truth. If a guy doesn't have the natural talents Bruce had, he can chip away all day and he isn't going to find what Bruce had.

"His problem as a teacher was that he could pass on his ideas, but not his talent, and you needed both for his philosophy to work."

In fact, there is evidence in plenty to suggest that Lee was amply aware of his pupils' limitations, and that he geared his lessons to them. James Coburn, for example, Lee once told an interviewer, was "... definitely not a fighter. Lover - yes! He is really a super-nice guy. Not only that, but he is a very peaceful man. He learns Martial Arts because he finds that it is like a mirror to reflect himself. I personally believe that all types of knowledge - I don't care what it is - ultimately means self-knowledge. And that is what he is after."

And the volatile Steve McQueen was summarised by his Martial Arts Sensei as "... very uptight. Steve is very highly strung. Now, he could be a very good Martial Artist. I hope that the Martial Arts will cool him down a little bit, maybe make him a little bit mellower and be more peaceful like Jim."

Were the lessons having this effect on McQueen so far? Lee shook his head sorrowfully, "No, definitely not yet. First, because of shooting schedules and all that he cannot have lessons on a regular basis. And secondly, he is still on the level of regarding it right now as an excitement, like his motorcycle and his sports car - some form of release of his anger, or whatever you name it."

And another time, commenting on McQueen's almost schoolboyish attitude toward Jeet Kune Do, Lee asked: "Steve's a nice guy. But why does he go so slack-jawed every time he sees me fight?"

Stirling Silliphant, whose age nearly barred him from entering Lee's select band of trainee warriors, soon discovered that Lee had embarked him on a course designed to elicit either a natural talent, or a speedy resignation. Silliphant was put through the loop and pulley leg-stretching apparatus, and before the jokes about Chinese torture had died down, found himself facing a wall lined with hand and foot tougheners such as rice, sand, and dried peas.

Silliphant was also confronted with the "giant mushy bag," which took up half of Lee's garage, and which his pupils would be told to kick a reasonable distance. It stood higher than a man and about eight feet wide, and simply absorbed power. "Like kicking a marshmallow bigger than you," said Silliphant.

There were also devices which hit his pupils back, non-passive, tensile cushions on springs whose degree of power could be altered to vary the fury of the return attack that Silliphant & Co. were expected to endure. Then there was the air shield, a form of padding to protect a pupil from another's punch. If Lee hit Silliphant while the latter held the air shield, he would simply be hurled across the room.

But when all was done, Lee had taught his pupils well and efficiently, and was pleased with their efforts. He once brought a Hong Kong fighter to observe Silliphant in training, and somehow the middle-aged scriptwriter found himself in a sparring ring with Lee's guest. Silliphant recalls: "I beat him, badly, which made Bruce glow with pride. The boy stormed out, angered with embarrassment, and would never talk to Bruce again. He just wasn't prepared for my improvisation, which Bruce taught, and he was unable to adjust to my ego, although I could adjust to his ego."

"'You ignored his formality,' Bruce told me, 'and just went in and hit him.' He taught us only to win, not to lose. He called Katas (which are graceful but apparently impractical exercises) 'vertical death.'"

Probably the most accurate and incisive analogy for Lee's teaching methods is to be found in another Zen story, which is about an old Japanese sword master called Bokuden.

Bokuden had a remarkable history and reputation, even in old age, and young men would frequently seek him out and beg him to teach them.

One such youth came to his door, and Bokuden agreed to give him a trial. So he sent the youth to the kitchen, and there assigned to him the most degrading of chores. The youth was in Bokuden's kitchen for a year, at the end of which time, seething with frustration and impatience, he went to the old teacher and insisted that lessons begin, hinting that he was being exploited for cheap labour, and that perhaps Bokuden was too old to teach.

Bokuden nodded, and agreed that lessons should commence. He sent the youth back to the kitchen. A day or two later, having heard no more from his teacher, the pupil was working at the sink when Bokuden, without a word or any warning, leapt out from a doorway and belaboured him heavily and painfully with the flat side of a large sword. Then the old man slipped away again.

This process continued, without any conversation taking place between the two, without any formal tuition. Bokuden would just appear suddenly and lay about the youth. Eventually, inevitably, the boy became sensitive to the imminence of these attacks, he became capable of detecting the faintest rustle in the undergrowth, the slightest patter of bare feet on tiles, and Bokuden found himself no longer able to take his pupil by surprise.

So he congratulated his pupil, and began teaching him the art of swordsmanship. The youth had learned that quality which Bruce Lee valued above others: directness, and he had learned it in the kind of practical manner that would have made Bruce Lee beam with wholehearted approval.

THE WISDOM OF BRUCE LEE

CHAPTER SIX

HOW TO MEASURE YOUR OPPONENT
Just How Good Are You?

"When an inferior man plans to injure a gentleman, his heart is cruel, his plans are well laid out, and his actions are firm; therefore the gentleman can seldom escape. When a gentleman intends to punish a lower person, his heart is kind, his plans are incomplete, and he cannot quite go the limit; therefore more often than not he himself is victimised by it."

— TUT TUT

HOW TO MEASURE YOUR OPPONENT
Just How Good Are You?

*"When an inferior man plans to injure a gentleman, his heart
is cruel, his plans are well laid out, and his actions are firm;
therefore the gentleman can seldom escape.
When a gentleman intends to punish a lower person, his heart
is kind, his plans are incomplete, and he cannot quite go the
limit; therefore more often than not he himself is victimised by it."*

- TUT TUT

As the most celebrated Martial Artist in the world, Bruce Lee was plagued by challengers. They came from many quarters: from rival instructors with a vested interest in proving their style to be more lethal than Jeet Kune Do; from young punks who refused to believe that Lee's cinematic fights were any more than stunts (and whose scepticism was frequently bolstered by a first glimpse of the diminutive Lee in the flesh); and from fighters simply out to knock the king of Kung Fu from his throne.

It is now legend, of course, that not one of these challengers was successful, and that most went home with their tails dragging on the ground. But while their constant presence rarely bothered the fighter in Lee, the philosopher in him was forced to come to terms with his extra cinematic contests. He frequently vacillated between a natural, cocky pride in his invincibility and a vague disgust with the more sordid aspects of frequently being obliged to beat the hell out of transparently inferior opponents, simply in order to justify his standing.

Not that fights only came to Lee later in life. As a kid, as we have seen, he hardly led a protected life, and it was opponents such as larger bullies that led him to develop his body and his fighting arts. Lee describes how older students would take advantage of his weakness at school: "Those bastards enjoyed overpowering us, and as we weakened they used to slap us on our chest and face. I got so mad one day that I decided to dish out the same medicine to them. I made a concentrated effort to develop my flowing energy. While attending class, I began to press my arm against the edge of the desk, and flowed my energy. One of the friendly senior students spent some time after workouts exercising with me. In a few months, I got my revenge, and did I dish it out to them I I really picked on them after that."

And outside school, on the streets of Hong Kong, teenage life was no bed of roses: "I was riding on this ferry late one night," remembered Lee, "and these two punks began to tease me. 'Are you a boy or a girl? You sure dress like a girl.' They kept taunting me, but

I kept my cool and didn't say a word. As soon as the ferry docked, I followed them ashore and kind of baffled them when I began to cuss and swear at them. The bigger guy came after me, but I kicked him in his shin before he could do anything. While he was jumping up and down, hollering in pain, I went for the other guy, but he took off like a frightened rabbit."

If that unorthodox but indisputably effective kick on the shin sounds like a bit of early Jeet Kune Do, it is certainly true that Lee based his style on the practicalities of street rough-houses. To be a dangerous fighter, he would tell friends: "You must have complete determination. The worst opponent you can come across is one whose aim has become an obsession. For instance, if a man has decided that he is going to bite off your nose no matter what happens to him in the process, the chances are that he will succeed in doing it. He may be severely beaten up but that will not stop him carrying out his original objective. That is the real fighter."

Such home truths were learned by Lee the hard way. Once, as the leader of a youth gang in Hong Kong, he was challenged by another teenage mobster to a fight with unusual rules: "We'll fight on a rooftop and the winner can toss the loser over," insisted his rival. Lee consented, and they climbed five stories to the top of an apartment block. As Lee was preparing, the other boy leaped at him without warning, kicking him in the eye and belabouring him ferociously. Lee recovered, and went on to break both his opponent's arms and fracture his femur, before deciding not to throw him to certain death but to phone for an ambulance instead. Such fights taught Bruce Lee that there can be no rules or artificial courtesy in a true contest.

When he arrived in California, full of himself and his fighting ability, anxious to communicate his street-fightin' style to the rest of the world, he found antagonism and opposition not so much in the native populace as in the rest of the Oriental community. The truth was, there were already many schools of the Martial Arts in the USA, and if Bruce Lee figured that another one was necessary, the founders of those other schools disagreed. Particularly as Lee seemed set on teaching his Martial Arts not only to Easterners, but also to Caucasians-thus breaking an ancient unwritten law.

One of the first experts to decide to put Lee in his place was a master from San Francisco's Chinatown called Wong Jack Man. Wong and his followers turned up at Lee's school one day with a challenge written on a scroll, informing Lee that if he lost the ensuing fight, he was either to close down his school or stop teaching Westerners.

Lee asked Wong if he had been forced into this action by his followers. "I'm representing these people here," admitted Wong. "OK, then," said Lee - to the surprise of the attendant Chinese, who had expected the younger man to concede in the face of Wong's reputation. Even Wong was shaken, and suggested that they simply spar lightly for a few minutes. But Lee was angered and serious.

"No," he insisted. "You challenged me, so let's fight."

"No hitting in the face. No kicking in the groin," said a worried Wong Jack Man. His objections were swept aside by Lee: "I'm not standing for any of that. You've come here with an ultimatum and a challenge, hoping to scare me off. You've made the challenge, so I'm making the rules. So far as I'm concerned, it's no-holds-barred. It's all-out."

Linda Lee, who was watching this scenario while eight months pregnant, reports that not for a moment did she feel at all worried for Lee's safety. "None of these men,"

THE WISDOM OF BRUCE LEE

she later wrote, "had any real inkling of how dangerous Bruce could really be." She was right. Within minutes, Wong's followers were trying to stop the fight, as Wong was ignominiously running from Lee. Lee hauled his sorry challenger to the ground and extracted a submission.

At another time, Lee was demonstrating Kung Fu at his university in Seattle. As he later described the scene: "While explaining the art is the forerunner of Karate, I was rudely interrupted by a black belt Karate-man from Japan who sat in front of the stage. 'No, no, Karate not from China. Come from Japan.'"

Lee, never one to tolerate interruption, let alone contradiction, put the black belt down with some sarcastic response. Later, the Karate-man approached him, seething, and demanded a fight "next week." "Why not now?" asked Bruce, casually, and they engaged in battle. Much to the Karate-man's chagrin, Lee completely outfought him, winning in seconds. "He was too slow and too stiff," the victor later recalled.

Lee credited an opponent with teaching him the limitations of Wing Chun, and finally turning him to Jeet Kune Do - but not because that opponent got the better of him. It was a fight in San Francisco, and after a minute or two his opponent began to run away. Lee gave chase, and, "Like a fool, I kept punching him behind his head and back. Soon my fists began to swell from hitting his hard head. Right then I realised Wing Chun was not too practical and began to alter my way of fighting."

While the world of the Martial Arts may have been a world fraught with tension and littered with potential enemies, Lee was soon to discover that the movies were no easy escape into unchallenged superiority. Many of the stuntmen that Lee came to work with were notable fighters in their own right, and what's more, they were not used to film stars who doubled as brilliant Martial Artists. Consequently Lee was regarded by many with scepticism, and called upon to prove himself. Proving himself was, luckily, something that came naturally to Bruce Lee. Stirling Silliphant tells a story about a fight scene which he got Lee to choreograph:

"There were a couple of stuntmen - big, tough Caucasian cats - assigned to the movie who were very sceptical about Bruce. They saw this 135-pound Chinese who, when he didn't want to look tough, could maintain a very low profile."

The stuntmen resented the fact that an outsider, a non-union man, had been put in charge of their fight scenes. They grudgingly obeyed Silliphant's orders to listen to Lee, but kept poking fun and dropping sarcastic comments. Finally, Silliphant took Lee to one side and suggested that he demonstrate a few of his skills to the men. Lee nodded, picked up an air shield, and offered it to one of the stuntmen.

"One of you guys," he said, "hold this shield. I'm going to give it a little kick. But I suggest you brace yourself first. I kick pretty hard."

The stuntman mockingly I agreed, and stood at the edge of a swimming pool holding the air shield. Without a run-up, or any kind of advance preparation or warning, Lee kicked him through the air into the pool. "That guy," comments Silliphant, "came up a Christian! From that moment on, he would have killed for Bruce."

His friend the second stuntman, however, was not quite convinced. He squatted where the first man had stood, and braced himself thoroughly. Without further ado, Lee gave him exactly the same treatment. The non-union choreographer had little trouble after that!

THE WISDOM OF BRUCE LEE

At another time, when Lee was actually starring in a fight scene himself, a Chinese youth sitting on a wall overlooking the set kept alternately challenging and insulting him, with cries of "phony" and "fake." Lee ignored the heckler for some time, and then, between takes, lost his patience. He called to the youth, "Come on, then, come and beat me up."

The challenger jumped down, and made for Lee. Bob Wall, who was on set at the time, recalled that the "kid was good. He was no punk. He was strong and fast, and he was really trying to punch Bruce's brains in. But Bruce just methodically took him apart. He slammed the kid into a rock wall, then trapped him with his right knee and left hand. He took the kid's hand, punched in, just touched his cheek, brought his hand back, and said, 'See, you're mine.'"

For several minutes, Lee humiliated the youth, trapping him helplessly, drawing a slight amount of blood from his mouth, eventually wearing down his opponent until the youth was too exhausted to move. Then Lee told him where he'd gone wrong.

"This is a lesson for you," he said, "I want you to understand. Look, your stance is too wide; you were doing this..."

At the end, the youth shook both Lee's hands before climbing back on his wall, and said: "You really are a master of the Martial Arts."

There were some in the movie business, of course, with more wisdom. They recog-

nised Lee's ability on first viewing, and would never have challenged him. James Coburn, for instance, regarded Lee as being above competition, quite simply outside the class of any other living fighter: "The first time I saw him, I had no doubt that he was the greatest Martial Artist that I had ever witnessed; probably one of the greatest of all time. And he knew it, too. I mean, it wasn't a question of him competing with anybody. It was a question of everybody else competing with him because he was like the beacon, the source of the energy that everybody got something from."

Lee himself, when asked by John (son of Gene) Tunney: "Could you have beaten my father?" smiled and replied: "To tell you the truth, I could beat anybody in the world. Of course, if I sat still and your father hit me, forget it. The question is: could he ever get close to me?"

Such awesome confidence (or was it just simple self-knowledge) never actually stopped the challenges, or the stories. Lo Wei, the Mandarin director of *The Big Boss* and *Fist of Fury* told the Hong Kong press after Lee had sacked him that Lee had gone for him with a knife. To Lee, such a story was beneath ridicule.

"If I had wanted to kill Lo Wei," he said, "I would not have used a knife. Two small fingers would have been enough."

In a late interview, conducted shortly before his death, Lee told radio Hong Kong about the pressures of being constantly challenged and pressed into action: "When I first learned the Martial Arts," he explained, "I too challenged many established instructors. But I have learned that challenging means one thing to you, it is 'What is your reaction to it? How does it get you?' Now, if you are secure in yourself, you treat it very lightly because you ask yourself: 'Am I really afraid of that man? Do I have any doubts that that man is going to get me?' And if you do not have such doubts and such fears, then I would certainly treat it very lightly, just as today the rain is coming down very strong but tomorrow the sun may come out again."

When it was pointed out to him that whatever the outcome of a challenge, the challenger could not lose because everyone expected Lee to win anyway, and his opponent was guaranteed plenty of free publicity, Lee shrugged such challenges off as irrelevant: "Well, let's face it, in Hong Kong today, can you have a fight? I mean a no-holds-barred fight? Is it legal? It isn't, is it? And for me, I am always the last to know about these challenges, man. I mean I always find out from newspapers, reporters, before I personally know what the hell is happening."

Finally, the inevitable question, posed to Lee as if he had not already answered it a hundred times in a hundred fights with a hundred different opponents. Echoing the kid on the wall, the stuntmen by the swimming pool, and Gene Tunney's son, an interviewer asked Lee, "Are you able to take care of yourself?" Lee laughed: "I will answer first of all with a joke, if you don't mind. All the time, people come up and say, 'Bruce, are you really that good?' I say, 'Well, if I tell you I'm good, probably you will say that I'm boasting. But if I tell you I'm no good, you'll know I'm lying. Okay, going back to being truthful with you, let's put it this way: I have no fear of an opponent in front of me. I am very self-sufficient, and they do not bother me. And should I fight, should I do anything, I have made up my mind that, baby, you had better kill me before I get you."

THE WISDOM OF BRUCE LEE

CHAPTER SEVEN

FILM AND REALITY?
The Fighter as Actor and Director

> "Humility is a good thing but over-humility is near to crookedness; silence is a virtue, but undue silence bespeaks a deceitful mind."
>
> - TUT TUT

FILM AND REALITY?
The Fighter as Actor and Director

"Humility is a good thing, but over-humility is near to crookedness; silence is a virtue, but undue silence bespeaks a deceitful mind."

-TUT TUT

"As an actor," wrote an English critic of *Fist of Fury*, "Bruce Lee makes a very good Martial Artist." It is a put-down that many people would echo, which is a pity, for it contains little more than a grain of truth. It is true that Lee had none of the range or delicacy of expression of Sir Laurence Olivier, it is difficult to imagine him making a good job of Hamlet, or Falstaff (although his Othello might have been interesting). But Lee understood movies. He knew why people went to the cinema probably better than Olivier, and he knew how to give the cinemagoer what the cinemagoer wanted. And even the most cursory examination of his thoughts on the subject indicate that much consideration and reappraisal had gone into them. Linda Lee was once surprised to hear her husband say that movies were not an art. "They are," he explained, "a combination of commercial creativity and creative commerce."

Lee had, of course, a theatrical family background. Apart from his own childhood parts in *Kid Cheung* and other Hong Kong films, his father Li Hoi-Chuen was lead comic singer for the Cantonese Opera. Lee later described his father's act as "one dimensional, but it's really stylised and very formal and very groovy indeed!"

More practically, Li Hoi-Chuen was able to advise his ambitious son about some of the rigors of show business: "My dad used to tell me to save my dough because he knew I wanted to be an actor. He would say, 'When you become an actor you can earn big money quickly, but when things are down you may not see any money for months. So save everything you can to stretch your money when you need it.'"

Lee did not waste the days spent without work. He spent them deciding what kind of work he'd deliver when he got the chance. Slipping into his old habit of jotting down thoughts in order to clarify them, he has left us with the following notes, introduced by him as "a sort of personal view of the motion picture industry and the ideas of an actor as well as a human being": "Above all," he went on, "I have to take responsibility to myself and do whatever is right. The script has to be right, the director has to be right, my time must be devoted to preparation of the role - after that comes money. To the business people in films - and I have to say that cinema is a marriage of art and business - the actor is not a human being but a product, a commodity. However, as a human being I have the right to be the best goddamn product that ever walked, and work so hard that the business people have to listen to me. You have that personal obligation to yourself to make yourself the best product available according to your own terms. Not the biggest or the most successful, but the best quality - with that achieved comes everything else."

Hence his great pleasure on reading the reviews of *Longstreet*, which could be described as his American screen breakthrough: "First time in my life that I ever had any kind of review for my acting," he beamed, "and I'm glad they were favourable." His notes continue, examining both his chosen profession and his own abilities: "An actor is, first of all, like you and me, a human being who is equipped with the capability to express himself psychologically and physically with realism and appropriateness, hopefully in good taste, which simply means the revelation of the sum total of all that he is - his tastes, his education, his individual uniqueness, his soul-searching experiences, his idiosyncrasies, etc. Just as no two human beings are alike, the same holds true for actors."

With such high-minded ideas and preconceptions, Bruce Lee entered the Mandarin film industry to make *The Big Boss*. He saw the job as vital: "*The Big Boss* was an important movie for me, because I had a starring role for the first time. I felt that I could do a better job than in The Green Hornet and I had more confidence as I had just done Longstreet."

But the level of professionalism in the Hong Kong movie industry appalled him. After boning up on what he was about to be asked to do by going to see "a whole bunch of Mandarin movies," he was shattered: "They were awful," he ruefully remembered. "For one thing, everybody fights all the time, and what really bothered me was that they all fought exactly the same way. Wow, nobody's really like that. When you get into a fight, everybody reacts differently, and it is possible to act and fight at the same time.

Most Chinese films have been very superficial and one-dimensional." To another listener he condemned them as "unreal - all that jumping around all the time!" and he told the American magazine *Black Belt*: "Everything is overplayed in Mandarin films. To make really good ones, you'd have to use subtlety, and very few people in the business want to risk any money by trying that." And the man who'd worked so appreciatively with a Stirling Silliphant screenplay in *Longstreet* added: "On top of which, the scripts are pretty terrible. You wouldn't believe the stuff I rewrote for **The Big Boss**. All of us have to come secondary to the quality of the film itself."

He was never completely satisfied with the screenplays he was given, insisting as each film came and went on greater control, and telling journalists: "The script is the most important thing. That is why I have always insisted on having a good script before accepting the role. Just recently I turned down a Golden Harvest film because I wasn't happy with the script. "At present I am working on the script for my next film. I haven't really decided on the title yet, but what I want to show is the necessity to adapt oneself to changing circumstances. The inability to adapt brings destruction. I already have the first scene in my mind. As the film opens, the audience sees a wide expanse of snow. Then the camera closes in on a clump of trees while the sounds of a strong gale fill the screen. There is a huge tree in the centre of the screen and it is all covered with thick snow. Suddenly there is a loud snap and a huge branch of the tree falls to the ground. It cannot yield to the force of the snow so it breaks. Then the camera moves to a willow tree which is bending with the wind. Because it adapts itself to the environment, the willow survives.

"It is this sort of symbolism which I think Chinese action films should seek to have. In this way I hope to broaden the scope of action films."

Not everybody in Hong Kong was motivated by such grand concepts, however, and all of Lee's discontent with the stale of his home film industry finally bubbled to the surface in an interview with the *Hong Kong Standard*. It is a fascinating glimpse into the cinematic mind of Bruce Lee, a mind that was developing faster than the mandarin industry itself, and which was eventually to leave Hong Kong behind. For the time, however, he contented himself with making it perfectly clear: "I'm dissatisfied with the expression of the cinematic art here in Hong Kong. It's time somebody did something about the films here. There are simply not enough soulful characters here who are committed, dedicated, and are at the same time professionals. I believe I have a role. The audience needs to be educated and the one to educate them has to be somebody who is responsible. We are dealing with the masses and we have to create something that will get through to them. We have to educate them step by step. We can't do it overnight. That's what I'm doing right now. Whether I succeed or not remains to be seen. But I just don't feel committed, I am committed.

"I didn't create this monster - all this gore in the mandarin films. It was there before I came. At least I don't spread violence. I don't call the fighting in my films violence. I call it action. An action film borders somewhere between reality and fantasy. If it were completely realistic, you would call me a bloody, violent man. I would simply destroy my

opponent by tearing him apart or ripping his guts out. I wouldn't do it so artistically. I have this intensity in me, the audience believes in what I do because I believe in what I do. But I act in such a way as to border my action somewhere between reality and fantasy.

"I can't express myself fully on film here, or the audiences wouldn't understand what I was talking about half the time. That's why I can't stay in Southeast Asia all the time. I am improving and making new discoveries every day. If you don't you are already crystallised and that's it." Bruce slashed his throat with his finger. "I'll be doing different types of films in the future, some serious, some philosophical, and some pure entertainment. But I will never prostitute myself in any way."

Fortunately for Lee, the man with whom he was to work on *The Big Boss* and, later, *Fist of Fury*, had no illusions about the quality of Hong Kong films. Indeed, when Raymond Chow had first gone to work for Run Run Shaw, the virtually omnipotent Mandarin movie mogul, and watched some of Shaw's films, his reactions had been uncannily similar to Lee's: "I was horrified," Chow says, "and told him (Shaw) I wanted to quit. I felt so appalled I felt sure I couldn't sell the film." But now Raymond Chow had left the old Mandarin in an atmosphere of rancour and suspicion, and had lifted Bruce Lee, Hong Kong's hottest property for years, from under Shaw's nose. Chow was anxious to keep Lee, anxious enough to allow the self-confident young actor such luxuries as the rewriting of his screenplays. Lee, however, was not yet satisfied. "Most Chinese movies followed the Japanese," he said, "and there were too many weapons - especially swords. So we used a minimum of weapons and made it *(The Big Boss)* into a better film."

He was quick to point out that the character in *The Big Boss* was not himself, and even to give credit to others in the moulding of the character and the film: "This is definitely a screen personality," he explained of the slow-to-anger hero of *The Big Boss*, "because as a person one thing that I have learned in my life - a life of self-examination, self-peeling bit by bit, day by day - is that I do have a bad temper. A violent temper, in fact. So that is definitely a screen personality, some person I am portraying, and not Bruce Lee as he is."

Asked about the brothel scene in *The Big Boss*, which caused some controversy in Hong Kong, Lee defended director Lo Wei's decision to include it: "Now the way I look at that, that was a suggestion of the director. I accept it in such a way which is, him being such a simple man (the hero, not Lo Wei!) when all of a sudden he has made up his mind he is going to go and either kill or be killed. It's kind of a sudden thing, the thought just occurs that, well, such is the basic need of a human being that I might as well enjoy it before I kick the bucket - like that kind of an attitude. It is just an occurrence, you know."

Linda Lee recalls that during the filming of the brothel scene in *The Big Boss*, just before Bruce was brought face to face with the naked prostitute, he leaned across the arc-lights and smiled whimsically at her. "Part of the fringe benefits," he whispered.

The success of *The Big Boss* throughout the world heartened Lee, and gave him hope for more than just his own career. He saw the box-office records that were being broken from Beirut to Buenos Aires as vindication of his ideals and movie philosophies. But he was modest enough to admit some surprise: "We knew from the outset that the film was going to be a success," he told the press, "but I have to admit we weren't really expecting it to be that successful. I hope that *The Big Boss* comes to represent a new trend in Mandarin cinema. I mean, people like films that are more than just one long-armed hassle. With any luck I hope to make multilevel films here - the kind of movies where you can watch the surface story if you like, or can look deeper into it. Most of the Chinese films to date have been very superficial and one-dimensional. I tried to do that in *The Big Boss*. The character I played was a very simple, straight-forward guy. Like, if you told this guy something, he'd believe you. Then, when he finally figures out he's been had, he goes animal. This isn't a bad character, but I don't want to play him all the time. I'd prefer somebody with a little more depth."

There is an apocryphal story which has been repeated and embroidered upon so many times as to be confusing, about Bruce's realisation that *The Big Boss* had finally made him a star. Lee's own version of that story is possibly the most reliable. It is certainly the most interesting: "I realised the potential of the movie when I attended the premiere. Bob Baker (from Stockton, California) was in town for a part in the second movie, Fist of Fury. He and I sat in the front seats without being noticed. As the movie progressed, we kept looking at the reactions of the fans. They hardly made any noise in the beginning, but at the end they were in frenzy and began clapping and clamouring. Those fans there are emotional. If they don't like the movie, they'll cuss and walk out. When the movie came to an end, Bob, almost in tears, shook my hand and said, "Boy, am I happy for you.""

The confidence in himself which had taken Lee so far, which had enabled him to convince others to back him in a film radically different from the run-of-the-mill Mandarin movies, was now justified and given room to develop. If the struggles of trying to make it to the top had frustrated Lee, stardom suited him. "People ask me as an actor, 'How good are you really in Kung Fu?'" he once said.

"I always kid them about that. If I tell them I'm good, they'll probably say I'm boasting, but if I tell them I'm no good I'm lying. I tell them to believe half of what they see and nothing that they hear - and remember, seven hundred million Chinese can't be Wong."

But the wit and charm were, as ever, only one side of the coin. Lee's urge was to be remembered as something more than just a box-office smash, a one or two-film wonder. He still searched within himself for some elusive definition of the kind of actor he yearned to be: "An actor is a dedicated being who works damn hard so that his level of understanding makes him a qualified artist in self-expression - physically, psychologically and spiritually. I regard acting as an art much like my practice in Martial Art because it is an expression of the self. "As an actor I am frustrated between business and art, with the hope that through harmonious reconciliation of these I can then come out expressing myself and truthfully communicating."

His newfound value as a screen property brought complications into his life. He discovered what he previously must only have suspected: that the movie business can be a cynical, cut-throat affair; with much money and few scruples. "Wary and slightly disillusioned, Lee decided to stay above it all: "I had a heck of a problem," he told *Fighting Stars* magazine. "I had people stop by my door and just pass me a check for $200,000. When I asked them what it was for they replied. 'Don't worry, it's just a gift to you.' I mean, I didn't even know these people, they were strangers to me. I was very, very confused, and totally suspicious of everyone, feeling I could trust nobody any longer. It was very bewildering - I even grew suspicious of my old pals. I was in a position where I didn't know who was trying to take advantage of me. When people pass out big money - just like that, you don't know what to think. I destroyed all those checks but it was difficult to do, because I

THE KUNG-FU MONTHLY ARCHIVE SERIES

didn't know what they were for. Sure, money is important in providing for my family, but it isn't everything."

So, several hundreds of thousands of dollars poorer, but feeling clean of soul, Lee was able to get on with the next Raymond Chow/Lo Wei/Bruce Lee production, *Fist of Fury*. His belief in himself by now quite justifiably knew no bounds. *Fist of Fury* would, he claimed: "... do for me what the spaghetti westerns did for Clint Eastwood. There is such an incredible amount of interest in the East since the visit of President Nixon that our films should find ready acceptance in the American market. I think we have what the US public wants - violence and humour. I mean, nobody can take seriously a scene in which a man is stabbed and his intestines come out and yet he picks them up, ties them around his waist and continues the fight. It's almost the kind of humour that the Bond films have."

Lee was to change his mind about *Fist of Fury*, indeed about those qualities that he had determined "the US public wants." He told the press: "I think it is unhealthy to play up violence. If a man has his throat slit during a fight, for example, the audience should not be given a frontal view of his blood-soaked throat.

"But it should be remembered that violence and aggression is part of everyday life now. You see it over the TV and in Vietnam. You can't just pretend that it does not exist. On the other hand, I don't think one should use violence and aggression as the themes of movies. The glorification of violence is bad. That is why I insisted that Chen Chen, the role I played in *Fist of Fury*, should die in the film. He had killed many people, and he had to pay for it."

And in an interview shortly before his death, that "basic need of a human being" that he had succumbed to in *The Big Boss* even came under fire. He was asked whether being in bed with a lovely young movie star in front of a camera crew intimidated him. Bruce Lee laughed: "Well, it certainly would not intimidate me. I can tell you that! It's all right as long as the script justifies it. But I definitely do not agree to putting something in there just for the heck of it, because that is exploitation. For instance, when I started shooting *The Big Boss*, the first question that was asked of the film was, 'How many thousands of feet of film is it going to be?' My first question was, why do I start fighting? You see what I am saying? It seems to be the thing now to go for sex and blood just merely for the sake of sex and merely for the sake of blood."

Essentially, he did not believe that the Hong Kong movie industry was good enough, inspired enough, or big enough for him. He had harboured an inferiority complex about the Mandarin business, ironical in one who was to give it a name for success, and a modicum of quality. Even while working on his third Mandarin film, *The Way of the Dragon*, Lee was complaining that his movies were not geared sufficiently for Western audiences, and insisting that they should not be released in the West. There is an element of apology in his comments, almost as if he is asking the West to have patience with him, he can do much better, given the opportunity.

"Raymond Chow," he said, "is keen on the idea (of dubbing The Big Boss and releasing it in London and Australia), but I'm personally not too happy. And it is not only the production, but the theme that I am talking about. You see, there is a cultural gap between the West and the East. What is good for the Westerners may not necessarily be good for the Easterners, and vice versa. Learning English, for example, is not too difficult.

But to understand the nuances of tones and the meaning of colloquial expressions, that is difficult.

"At present, most of our Chinese films are geared toward the Southeast Asian audience. People here have different tastes from those of people who live in the West. We have to try to produce films with universal appeal if we are to gain international recognition. That is what I intend to achieve in my future films."

And the *China Mail* was told that Mandarin film bosses had the wrong idea about his ambitions: "They think I am only interested in money. That's why they all try to lure me onto their sets by promising me huge sums and nothing else. But at heart I only want a fair share of the profit." Almost plaintively, Lee concluded, with these words: "What I long for is to make a really good movie."

But at the time, he considered *The Way of the Dragon* to be his best yet, and a good enough film within its obvious limitations of plot and characterization, which Lee summarised concisely enough: "It's really a simple plot of a country boy going to a place where he cannot speak the language, but somehow he comes out on top because he honestly and simply expresses himself by beating the hell out of everyone else!"

And a curious reporter on set was told by Lee that his new part was: "... a simple man, but he likes to act big, you see. He doesn't really understand a metropolis like Rome, but he pretends that he does. He doesn't want to appear the country bumpkin, so rather than admit his ignorance of the language to the Italian waitress he merely points to the menu to order. The result is that he ends up with five bowls of soup."

Behind the scenes, however, *The Way of the Dragon* had a different, more complex plot. For the first time, Lee was coproducing the film with Raymond Chow, and directing it himself. He had ousted Lo Wei, and revelled in his new responsibilities: "I worked almost around the clock for days and lost several more pounds. I did it because it was fun. It was something I had always had ah interest in. I got hold of a dozen books on film production and direction and really dug into them."

He wasted no time in informing the world of his intentions. The future seemed, at last, to be charted satisfactorily: "I want to direct more films. Directing, I feel, is more creative. You really get a chance to produce the result you want. An actor is restricted. He can only do as the director instructs. In my case I could influence the director to a certain extent because of my status, but it was not a satisfactory state of affairs because I knew I was interfering and I hate to interfere with other people's work."

So, the discomfort of having to interfere with Lo Wei's direction gone, how thoroughly was he going to throw himself into his work?

"I feel that it would not be fair to anyone if I started shooting a dozen films a year. I couldn't possibly give any of the films the full attention and concentration that it requires. I want to limit the number of films which I appear in each year. These tempting offers are making life more and more complicated."

It seemed, then, that Lee had reconciled himself with the Mandarin industry. He need never be directed by another person again, he could limit his output as he pleased, and was proud of his latest product. When he told the press that *The Way of the Dragon* would gross more than five million Hong Kong dollars (more than twice *The Sound of Music*), they mocked. "This film is different," he said. It was, and it did gross more than HK$5,000,000. Michael Kaye, who worked as Lee's English voice-dub, saw Lee's originality at work: "Normally in a Chinese movie, you don't honour your enemy - you wipe him out in the ghastliest possible way with the most blood and gore, and you enjoy doing it. But in *The Way of the Dragon*, Lee was beginning to work out something else, a style that said, 'Let's be proud to be Chinese, but at the same time honour your enemy.'"

But the kind of praise that was now coming Lee's way, unique as it was for Mandarin films, was still insufficient to satisfy him. He wanted the prestige that he was now sure only Hollywood could provide. A frustrating blow came when he heard that his old friend, script-writer Stirling Silliphant was going ahead at Twentieth Century Fox with *The Silent Flute*, a film idea that Bruce, Stirling, and James Coburn had worked out together in the old, pre-stardom days. Bruce was mortified, and called Silliphant on the telephone: "Who will you get to replace me?" he asked. "Who could play five parts?" (In the original concept, Lee was to have done just that - play five roles in the film!)

Silliphant, accustomed to and patient with his friend's excitable temperament, tried to calm Lee: "As a matter of fact, we're getting five actors to replace you, and if you were to rejoin the project, I was going to suggest that you only play one role. Playing five roles would be old Hollywood Lon Chaney stuff."

But Lee was not to be reconciled. In a fit of pique, he told Silliphant: "You can't afford me, anyway. I get a million dollars a picture now."

His yen to make it to the studios of Hollywood was naturally reflected in his relationships with Chow and the Hong Kong studios. They became strained and unhappy, a situation perfectly summarised by Lee's reaction to an article published in a fan magazine on Chow and Lee's working relationship. Lee responded touchily: "The article," he stormed, "puts forth a notion that I am a brainless child who relies solely on Raymond. But I am not. I am my own boss, and I have as many brains as anyone else."

Even the work-rate of the Hong Kong industry (which is usually noted for its phenomenal rate of production) came under fire, Idling around a set one morning, he confided in a journalist: "Everyone knows that we start work at nine. It is 9:30 now. The director, myself, is here, but my workers have not arrived. This sort of thing is unheard of in the States. Part of the reason these people are late is that it is the fashion for other big stars and directors to be late. A problem with the Hong Kong film industry is that there are too many stars and too few actors. Box-office popularity often provides the stars with considerable power, unfortunately many tend to misuse it."

Finally, of course, and inevitably, he got to work with the Hollywood studios that, just a year or two before, he had been sure had rejected him. And if the Mandarin industry had found him a little edgy and inclined to intolerance of late, his co-workers on the Warner Bros, set of *Enter the Dragon* could hardly have been more impressed with his patience and expertise. Jim Kelly remembers: "Bruce gave me respect as a Martial Artist to do whatever I wanted to do. He didn't say, 'Jim, this is what you're going to do. That's it!' Before we even got into the fight scenes, which he choreographed, he said, 'Jim, I want you to do what you want to do. I know that you did your technical advising on Melinda. You know your art, and you can do whatever you want to do. I'll give you any help you want. But if you want to do your own fight scenes, I'll leave it up to you to do whatever you want to do.'

"So I did the fight scene in the stadium myself. Bruce had something laid out, and he said, 'Jim, do you like this?' I said 'I may change this and that.' But it wasn't, 'Hey Jim, this is it! You got to do it because I'm Bruce Lee. I'm the technical adviser.' It wasn't that type of thing."

And Bob Wall, another established, respected Martial Artist, also found Lee's flair, imagination, and friendly assistance of immense help: "It was always exciting to work with him because he was always teaching you something. Maybe you'd be busy trying to learn how to take a punch or a kick or something, and you wouldn't be paying attention to the camera. He'd say, 'Look, there are so many things to observe. Don't just get hung up on one thing.' He was always spouting philosophy, and he was stimulating."

Wall has another story which indicates clearly the kind of disciplined study and long hours of practice that Lee had put into perfecting his cinematic skills and techniques: "Bruce taught me how to take a punch on screen. He said, 'OK, I'm going to throw a punch. I want you to react to it.' When he threw the punch, I turned my shoulders and my head and my neck stiff because I had never thought about it. This is something most people have never thought about. I've never seen anyone do it naturally. It's just a very unnatural movement - to pretend you've just been hit violently and to time it. Bruce taught me how to relax my body, how to bend my knees and get up on my toes a little bit. He said, 'Imagine you're being hit. Think about it. What does it feel like? Feel It. Feel what you're doing. He had me relax and stand in front of a mirror and snap my head until my neck was so sore I could hardly whip it for a week."

Enter the Dragon could not have failed in Lee's eyes. He had invested in it too much expertise, experience, and hard work and too many hopes. It was going to be exactly right. When Fred Weintraub of Warners congratulated Lee on getting his

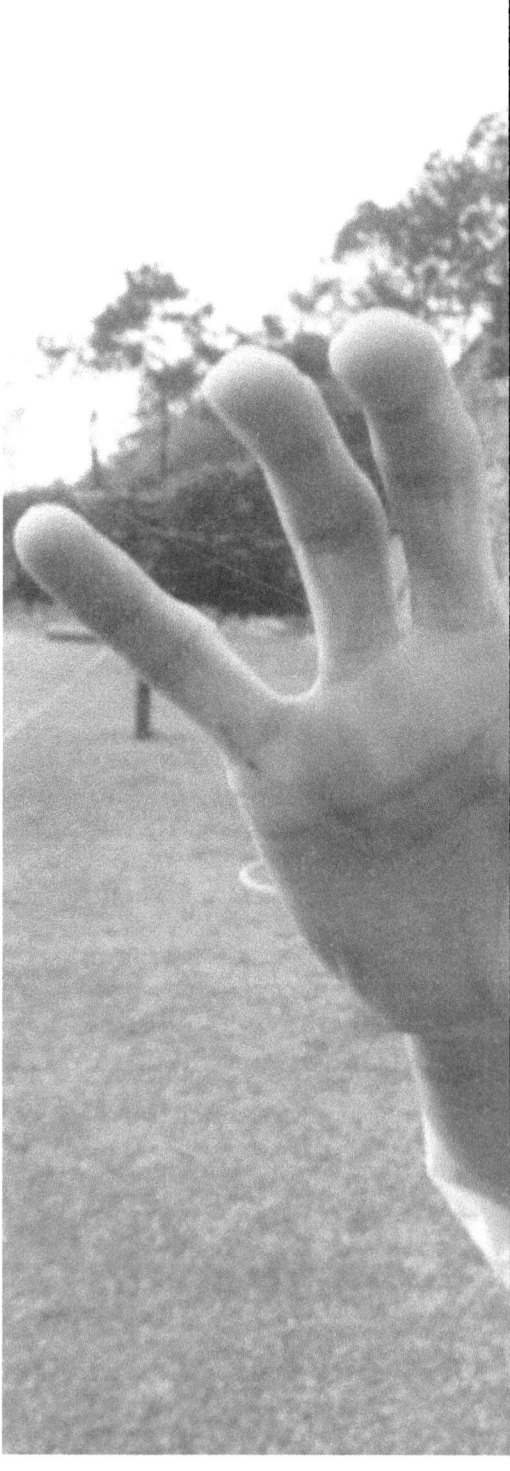

THE WISDOM OF BRUCE LEE

action scenes so nearly perfect on the first take, Lee explained why he was taking such care - with a smile dancing around his lips: "I've put a lot of my own money in this movie and each repeat shot is lost money. We're saving a bundle by eliminating the need to reshoot. I've got a vested interest in savings like that."

"This," he decided on the film's completion, "is definitely the biggest movie I ever made. This is the movie that I'm proud of because it is made for America as well as Europe and the Orient I'm excited to see what will happen, I think it's going to gross $20,000,000 in the US." He never did live to "see what will happen."

Enter the Dragon was the last completed film that Bruce Lee left, the last real chance to see how far his enormous cinematic talents had progressed from the days when, as a hopeful young fighter with a superb physique and unconquerable ambition, he had written: "Dedication, absolute dedication, is what keeps one ahead - a sort of indomitable obsessive dedication and the realisation that there is no end or limit to this because life is simply an ever-growing process, an ever-renewing process.

"An actor, a good actor that is, is an artist with depth and subtlety. Indeed, what the audience sees on the screen is the sum total of what that particular human being's level of understanding is. If he is ready, well-prepared, radiating a tremendous force of energy, an honest confidence of expression, working hard to grow and expand oneself in one's own process; well, this person is a professional, an 'efficient deliverer' in my book."

From what we know of his last film, *Game of Death*, of which only about thirty minutes of film were ever shot with him, the efficiency of Lee's delivery, as actor and director, had not decreased. Co-star Danny Inosanto has said of working with Lee on *Game of Death*: "Bruce was the most intensive worker I've ever seen. One rule on set was always to give Bruce your full attention. There just wasn't any other way to do things. He moved at such a rapid rate that it flabbergasted me. Bruce demanded perfection. Like the silent directors, Bruce talked and directed all through the scene. He could do that because the films are all shot without sound, and dubbed later.

He was very reassuring, very careful, very painstaking in his approach to the actor, to the problem of the scene, and to getting the results he wanted. Bruce never forgot, nor lost sight of, one single detail, no matter how small. And that attitude shows in all of his work."

If Lee's direction was a guide to the Catholicism of his talents and interests, though, it is by his own screen performances that he will be remembered. Here, his level of success is better summarised by another English critic, Verina Glaessner, than by the sceptic quoted at the beginning of this chapter. Miss Glaessner has written: "Lee is outrageous. He is often very funny and more than a bit of a ham. In his films he is a superlative fighter, a balletic exponent of a deadly art, in which it is impossible to separate the deadliness from the art. He didn't have to know how to act, he had something else that for many people transformed ordinary material into the charismatic - a sense of precarious" passivity in which the passivity is nothing more than a thin veil over the dangerous. His image swings constantly between that of the little boy who upset the apple cart and the bone-hard body fanatic. Probably the truth lay somewhere between the two."

Had Bruce Lee lived to read those words, he must have seen confirmed once and for all that his "indomitable obsessive dedication" had delivered the goods. Efficiently.

THE WISDOM OF BRUCE LEE

THE KUNG-FU MONTHLY ARCHIVE SERIES

CHAPTER EIGHT

THE HOLLYWOOD HERO
Dynasties and Dragons

"The tree that brushes the heavens grew from the tiniest sprout. The most elegant pagoda, nine stories high, rose from a small pile of earth. The journey of a thousand, miles began with but a single step."

- LAO TZU

THE HOLLYWOOD HERO
Dynasties and Dragons

"The tree that brushes the heavens grew from the tiniest sprout. The most elegant pagoda, nine stories high, rose from a small pile of earth. The journey of a thousand, miles began with but a single step."

- LAO TZU

Bruce Lee's relationship with that cultural enigma Hollywood is best described as short, productive, and turbulent. Determined to avoid the ancient role of the Oriental in Western films - the coolie, houseboy, or shifty deviant - Lee approached Hollywood with a justified scepticism. As Stirling Silliphant put it: "Some of the struggles Bruce had while getting really heavily involved in films read like a scene out of any really grim fight against prejudice. Bruce would never play the chop-chop pigtail coolie. Everyone admired him for that. He insisted on being human."

Everyone may have admired him, but in the early days anyway, not everyone was prepared to give him the kind of work that he wanted. Looking back, Lee remembered: "When I went back to the States, I said, 'Here I am, a Chinese, not prejudiced or anything, just realistic. How many times in Hollywood films is a Chinese required? And when it is required, it is always branded as the typical tung-dung-tung-tung-tung, with the little pigtail in back. You know the type. So I said the hell with it.'"

While such blasé dismissals of anything Hollywood had to offer may have thrilled his Hong Kong following at a later date, they were far from truly representative of Bruce Lee's ambitions in the last years of the 1960s. Even during the filming of *The Big Boss*, Lee waited anxiously on a decision from Warner Bros, about his part in a projected series called *The Warrior*. He even boasted nervously to friends: "Warner Bros, has full confidence in me, and wants to have things done as planned. I was a little worried, because a series like this means all kinds of work, like 365 days a year. But finally I said, 'I'm gonna do the series one way or the other - damn the torpedoes, full speed ahead,' and I decided to plunge right in."

Warners shelved *The Warrior*, for reasons which Lee was convinced were essentially racist. Resorting to the Chinese puns that he occasionally used against himself, he commented: "I guess they weren't ready for a Hop-a-long Wong." But the rejection went deeper than he allowed himself to show. When a friend suggested that "circumstances" might be getting in his way, Lee exploded, "To hell with circumstances. I will make circumstances." And privately he noted down the way in which these circumstances would be made, on a piece of paper later uncovered by Linda: "I, Bruce Lee, will be the highest paid Oriental superstar in the United States. In return I will give the most exciting performances and render the best of quality in the capacity of an actor. Starting 1970, I will achieve world fame and from then onward till the end of 1980 I will have in my possession $10,000,000. I will live the way I please and achieve inner harmony and happiness."

As Linda points out, nobody could accuse him of being wise after the event. At the time, however, such predictions were laughable. Apart from anything else, there was an immense psychological battle to be won before any Chinese actor could consider themselves suitable for Hollywood. Bruce Lee expressed it perfectly: "To most (Oriental) people," he explained, "including the (Mandarin) actors and actresses, Hollywood is like a magic kingdom. It's beyond everyone reach."

Never one to let his sense of humour desert him, Lee found time to pass gently sarcastic comments on Hollywood. Desperate for work, he was led to believe at one time that the part of *Charlie Chan's Number One Son* was coming his way. Lee grinned at the irony: "That's what Chinese actors do for a living in Hollywood, isn't it? Charlie himself is always played by a round-eye wearing six pounds of make-up."

Perhaps he should not have mocked. Being considered for the *Number One Son* led to greater things, as Lee himself later recalled: "Just about the time I discovered that I didn't really wait to teach self-defence for the rest of my life, I went to the Long Beach International Karate Tournament and got myself discovered by Hollywood. That night, I received a phone call at my hotel for a try-out. Early next morning I stopped by 20th Century Fox and was hired to be Charlie Chan's new *Number One Son*. While I was attending a quickie one-month private crash-course in acting, the producer changed his mind and decided that I would be Kato instead."

Kato, the quick-fisted Robin to Britt Reid's *Batman* in the series *The Green Hornet*, turned out to be Lee's breakthrough part. But he was still not content, not reassured that Hollywood had a place for a talented Chinese; most of all he was not positive that the part was right for Bruce Lee, "Oriental superstar." He alleged, "Film producers in Hollywood thought they could make use of my Martial Art and hoped that I would act in their films. The Green Hornet is one of the examples in which I was being made use of. I discovered at that time acting in that kind of film was meaningless because the roles didn't fit me. That didn't mean that I could not play such roles, but that the situation only occurred because of my yellow face."

Later, he decided that the tint of his skin was not the only reason for his landing the part of Kato. He told a reporter: "You know the reason why I got that job? Well, the hero's name was Britt Reid. And I was the only Chinaman in all California who could pronounce 'Britt Reid.'"

Yet Lee was still set on superstardom - and not just plain, common-or-garden superstardom. He told Stirling Silliphant that he would be bigger than his two friends and pupils, McQueen and Coburn. Silliphant knew better than to laugh, but told him that it could never be, that he was "a Chinese in a world run by white men." If Lee took any real notice of Silliphant's pessimism, which is unlikely, it was because by now he had acted a part in one of Stirling's screenplays, in Longstreet, and liked it: "I played a Chinese boxing instructor who was grooming this blind dude for a really important street fight, and I had this really wonderful piece of Stirling Silliphant script to work from. That man is the greatest screenwriter of all time and he wrote me a beautiful monologue. You want to hear it? 'Listen, man, you can't see but you can hear. Listen to the wind. The wind. Listen to the birds. Can you hear them? You have to become the wind. Empty your mind, man. You know how water fills a cup. You have to be ready, man. You have to think about nothing. You have to become fluid. You have to become nothing.'"

There can be no doubt that the faith of friends like Stirling Silliphant helped Lee through those early days when Hollywood had its back turned and success seemed far away. Lee and Silliphant developed a unique relationship. Silliphant even wrote the screenplay for what was to be Lee's first starring part, a film called *The Silent Flute*. Some of the words seem admirably suited: "I'm not even sure what trials I passed through - or how I came to be here. I still have doubts, many doubts - how, without more struggle, can I resolve them?"

As it turned out, Lee's doubts were finally resolved when he had almost given up on Hollywood as a bad job - and it had something to do with a Silliphant screenplay. While Lee was in Thailand shooting *The Big Boss*, *Longstreet* had opened in the States. The incredible happened - Paramount, impressed by the response to Lee's performance in *Longstreet*, went looking for him. And poetic justice applied - the man who had camped on their doorstep for the last decade was nowhere to be found. Lee explains: "They couldn't get in touch with me because I was really in the sticks. We were so far out that we couldn't even get meat. I had only vegetables and rice, and I lost ten pounds."

When Paramount finally caught up with an undernourished Bruce Lee, wanting him to do regular *Longstreet* appearances, they discovered the boot to be on the other foot. Lee was now in demand and he relished it. Hollywood tasted some of its own medicine.

"I was getting offers from MGM and Warner Bros.," Lee blithely pointed out, "and didn't want to be tied to a long contract."

At the time of The Warrior, Lee had criticised Hollywood in the following words: "What's holding things up now is that a lot of people are sitting around in Hollywood trying to decide if the American television audience is ready for an Oriental hero. We could get some really peculiar reactions from places like the Deep South."

By the time that *The Big Boss* had made its startling impact on the movie business, the last thing that Hollywood could be accused of in its attitude towards Bruce Lee was hesitation. Now it was Lee's turn to choose his time. He decided on Warners, and between them the prestigious Hollywood company and the young Chinese star embarked on the making of *Enter the Dragon*. Ted Ashley, Chairman of Warner Bros., had always struck Lee as being a fair-minded businessman, and the following letter, written to Ashley upon the completion of *Enter the Dragon*, explains much of Lee's new-found relationship with Hollywood: "Ted, nowadays, my offers for doing a film have reached a point which I guarantee will both surprise as well as shock you. Viewing from the angle of efficient practical business sense, I hope we will be fair and square and have mutual trust and confidence - I have had a bad experience doing a picture with some person or organisation in Hong Kong. In other words, I was burned once, and didn't like it.

"My twenty years of experience, both in Martial Arts and acting, has apparently led to the successful harmony of appropriateness of showmanship and genuine, efficient, artful expression. In short, this is it and ain't nobody knows it like I know it. Pardon my bluntness, but that is me!

"Under such circumstances, I sincerely hope that you will open up the genuineness within you and be absolutely fair and square in our transactions. Because of our friendship, I am holding up my money-making time - like ten offers from hungry producers - to look forward to this meeting. You see, Ted, my obsession is to make, pardon the expression, the fuckingest action motion picture that has ever been made.

"In closing, I will give you my heart, but please do not give me your head only; in return, I, Bruce Lee, will always feel the deepest appreciation for the intensity of your involvement."

In kicking down the sign forbidding Chinese from the park in *Fist of Fury*, Lee had unequivocally dramatised his statement that the Chinese were no longer the "Sick Men of Asia." By striking such deals and cementing such relationships with Warner Bros., he was now making it clear that they were no more the invalids of Hollywood. Ashley wanted Lee to do five films, to which, Lee said, and "told me they would not pay a million dollars for my services but they could make other lucrative arrangements." As it turned out, Warners would have been obliged to pay him rather more than a million. *Enter the Dragon* was, after *My Fair Lady*, the company's second biggest money-maker of all time.

Stirling Silliphant points to the achievement: "Bruce was more than just a single success story. He represented a whole race finally being accepted in films."

Raymond Chow emphasises it: "Now the door is open, it is easier for distributors to be receptive to the idea of Chinese films. You have no idea of the trouble we ran into when we first started to push our films overseas. The reaction was: 'What! A Chinese film!' Then Bruce Lee changed all that."

And Lee himself was happy enough to be "the highest paid Oriental superstar in the United States." Hollywood and he had made their peace. Laughingly, he explained: "I have great confidence in the studio - I think it will outlive me."

THE WISDOM OF BRUCE LEE

CHAPTER NINE

SWEET IMPRISONMENT
Success and Stardom

"You may do good without thinking about fame, but fame will come to you never-the-less. You may have fame without aiming at riches, but riches are sure to follow in its wake. You may be rich without wishing to provoke emulation and strife, yet emulation and strife will certainly result. Hence the superior man is very cautious about how he does good."

— LIEH TZU

SWEET IMPRISONMENT
Success and Stardom

"You may do good without thinking about fame, but fame will come to you never-the-less.
You may have fame without aiming at riches, but riches are sure to follow in its wake.
You may be rich without wishing to provoke emulation and strife, yet emulation and strife will certainly result.
Hence the superior man is very cautious about how he does good."

- LIEH TZU

In an earlier chapter, we have said that stardom suited Bruce Lee. It did, and that is not to say that he was the model celebrity, a paragon of excellence in his handling of adulation and wealth, for he was not. But unlike some of similar fortune, Lee never regretted his fame. He accepted that he had worked to achieve it, and that the niggling discomforts and inconveniences that it caused were to be accepted cheerfully alongside the smoother benefits of financial security and professional freedom. International fame can work curious havoc on a person's state of mind, but Lee never allowed himself to be obviously affected by such pressures, although there is an argument to be made for the thesis that stardom's rigors drove him to his grave.

Above all, though, his thoughts and comments on the subject of his own and other people's fame are of interest because Bruce Lee became a greater celebrity quicker than anybody else this century, and because behind this meteoric rise was an agile, analytical mind.

Lee was driven by two primary urges: the first was to perfect whatever he took upon himself to study (i.e., the Martial Arts and moviemaking) ; the second was to have that perfection recognised. Fellow Martial Artist Jhoon Rhee recalls how in 1968, Lee told him: "Jhoon, within five years, I am going to make myself the biggest and highest recognised actor as well as Martial Artist."

And in 1970, he confided that he had visited an astrologer in Las Vegas: "She predicted that 1971 will be my year. But I've already had this feeling that my time for success is here. I can just about taste it."

In fact, by 1971 Lee had already tasted enough success to satisfy most people; and suffered enough of its unfortunate by-products to scare some away. His role as Kato in

THE KUNG-FU MONTHLY ARCHIVE SERIES

The Green Hornet had attracted to him an enthusiastic, if over-demonstrative following: "It can be a terrifying experience sometimes," said the most lethal Martial Artist in the world. "After a personal appearance at Madison Square Garden at a Karate tournament, I started to make an exit through a side door, escorted by three Karate men. I was practically mobbed outside, and I had to leave through another side door. And in Fresno, California, I was scratched, kicked, and gouged by riotous fans - I just couldn't protect myself!"

In later life, he unhesitatingly gave that part, Kato, the credit for setting him on the road to fame - not only in the USA, but also in Hong Kong. Especially in Hong Kong, in fact, for it was during a promotional visit for *The Green Hornet* in the colony that the Hong Kong public and press became charmed by him. When he returned to America, the Hong Kong media kept in touch: "One day," Lee once related with a bemused smile, "I got a long distance call from Hong Kong's largest newspaper. They asked me if I was still alive. 'Guess who you're talking to?' I replied. 'Nope, I haven't gotten into a fight.' 'But it's headlined in all the newspapers here that you were killed by some ruffians,' the dumbfounded reporter told me."

And, in a less bizarre vein, Hong Kong radio would call for friendly chats: "Those guys used to call me early in the morning and even kept a conversation going on the air so the public was listening to me. Then, one day, the radio announcer asked me if I wanted to do a movie there. When I replied that I would, if the price was right, I began to get calls from producers in Hong Kong and Taiwan."

One of the calls was from Raymond Chow, and it was his offer that Lee accepted. He was still convinced that America had made him - when asked in Hong Kong later what was the cause of his success, he replied: "My twelve years of preparation in the States. Without them I would be little different from the others here. I was in the US in my formative years and I think I learned a lot there. Another important factor," he added to be on the safe side, "is the great interest I have in my work. I am willing to give 101 percent attention to my films. And partly, I suppose, the audience senses the animation in me."

Yes, he still acknowledged his debt to Western training, but he now considered that Hong Kong was the proper launching pad for his trip to superstardom. Or was he just consoling himself after that rankling rejection by Warners in *The Warrior*? "I'm going to follow in the steps of Clint Eastwood and Charles Bronson," is what he promised an acquaintance. "They became famous by going to Europe. I'm going to do it by going to Hong Kong." The acquaintance laughed, and Lee's resolve was undoubtedly hardened.

As we have chronicled elsewhere, he realised that the holy grail of international stardom was his for the taking firstly when Paramount tried to get hold of him during the shooting of *The Big Boss* in Thailand ("The producers thought I was an important star. My prestige must have increased three times.") and secondly during the ecstatically received premiere of *The Big Boss*. At first, the material comforts amused and delighted him - he'd seen too little of them in the past: "Having money doesn't solve all your problems," he chuckled to *Fighting Stars* magazine, "but it sure beats not having any money."

But he gradually came to realise that money could be an entrapment to restricting the "honest expression" that he valued so dearly: "There is this group of people who try to utilise me for their own ends. There was this producer who insisted that I go along to see the rushes of his new film. To oblige him, I did. The next thing I know advertisements

THE WISDOM OF BRUCE LEE

for the film proclaimed in bold print that Bruce Lee had spoken highly of the production!"

And, despite being offered HK$250,000 for a momentary appearance, he decided to shun advertising. But even his own feature films, it appeared, could be restricted by Lee's stardom: "The box-office success of my first two films for Golden Harvest has given me a certain amount of manoeuverability. I can do what I like usually in a film. But it has also set certain limitations. People expect me to fight, you know. They expect action from me. So in a way, I am imprisoned by my own success."

The imprisonment, of course, extended outside the movie lots. Hong Kong is a cramped community. There are not many places for a sought-after individual to hide, as Lee realised soon enough: "I don't feel like social gatherings. Nor am I interested in publicising myself. But such things are unavoidable in a star's life, particularly in a small place like Hong Kong."

And he poured out his heart to his old Martial Arts friends from Black Belt magazine: "The biggest disadvantage is losing your privacy. It's ironic, but we all strive to become wealthy and famous, and once you're there, if s not all rosy. There's hardly a place in Hong Kong where I can go to without being stared at or people asking me for autographs. That's one reason I spend a lot of time at my house to do my work. Right now, my home and the office are the most peaceful places. I avoid parties. I don't drink or smoke and those events are many times senseless. I'm not that kind of cat. I don't like to wear stuffy clothes and be at places where everyone is trying to impress each other. Now, I'm not saying I'm modest. I rather like to be around a few friends and talk informally about such things as boxing and the Martial Arts. Whenever I go to such places as a restaurant, I try to sneak in without being detected. I'll go directly to a corner table and quickly sit down, facing the wall so my back is to the crowd. I keep my head low while eating. No, I'm not crazy. I only look like it.

"You see, if I'm recognised, I'm dead, because I can't eat with the hand that I have to use to sign autographs. And I'm not one of those guys that can brush people off. Now I understand why stars like Steve McQueen avoid public places. In the beginning I didn't mind the publicity I was getting. But soon it got to be a headache answering the same questions over and over again, posing for photos and forcing a smile."

And to his wife, Lee almost despairingly confided: "It's like I'm in jail. I'm like a monkey in the zoo. People looking at me and things like that, and basically I like simple life and I like to joke a lot and all those things. But I can't speak as freely as before, because misinterpretation comes in and all kind of things, you know.

"It hasn't changed me basically, because I know that in my process of being born and going to die something happened which is breaking some records. To me it doesn't mean anything. It's just something that happens. It's not that I'm prouder or better than I ever was, I'm just the same damn old shit."

As that last paragraph indicates, Lee was beginning to come to terms with his situation. It was necessary that he did so, in order to preserve both his domestic and professional life, as well as his sanity. He reasoned that the nature of fame in modern times was an artificial one: "The best carpenter," he commented, "is just as important as the man who's made an important film."

He dismissed the trappings and flatteries of celebrity: "Awards or trophies are just ornaments. Who needs them?"

And he fought to keep his life in perspective, to remember where he had come from, even keeping an old pair of broken spectacles in his Kowloon offices: "to remind me of the days when I was so broke I couldn't even afford a pair of new glasses."

Perhaps most importantly, though, he maintained the old friendships and relationships that he valued as tried and true, even going out of his way to re-establish contact with those that he feared might drift out of his orbit. Taky Kimura was one such friend. He was surprised one day to receive a telephone call from Lee, saying: "Look, I'm the same

THE WISDOM OF BRUCE LEE

guy I've always been. If there is ever anything you need, just ask me."

Mito Uyehara, publisher of *Black Belt* magazine, received the following letter, itself a fascinating document for its reflection of a man struggling to reconcile great ambition and success with a personal philosophy which called for modesty and inner calm: "To many, the word 'success' seems to be a paradise, but now that I'm in the midst of it, it is nothing but circumstances that seem to complicate my innate feelings toward simplicity and privacy. Yet, like it or not, circumstances are thrust upon me and, being a fighter at heart, I sort of fight it in the beginning but soon realise what I need is not inner resistance and needless conflict in the form of dissipation; rather, by joining forces, to readjust and make the best of it.

"I can't go wrong because what I've always liked in myself is this 'stickability' toward quality and the sincere desire to do it right. In a way, I am glad that this preposterous happening is occurring to me when I am maturing to a state of readiness and definitely will not blow it because of 'self-glorification' or being 'blinded by illusions,' I am prepared.

"Well, my dear friend - lately 'friend' has come to be a scary word, a sickening game of watchfulness toward offered friendship - I miss you and our once simple lunches together and our many joyful communications.

"Take care and have fun - hope you are still jogging, which is the only form of relaxation to me these days."

There were still times, however, when his ego, stroked and nourished by the sycophants that he simply could not avoid, seemed to break out, and express itself in ways that Lee would later regret. When Stirling Silliphant contacted him about their proposed film with James Coburn, *The Silent Flute*, he happened to find Lee in a churlish mood: "Why should I carry Coburn on my shoulders?" he asked, and while Silliphant gasped, started to attack him for studying Karate (rather than Jeet Kune Do). "Japanese Karate?" spat Lee, "how could you do it?" And when Silliphant came back on to the subject of James Coburn, Lee said dismissively: "I'm the star, not him."

When the failed James Garner film that Lee had taken a small part in, Marlowe was re-released in Hong Kong with Lee billed as the star, he took a most immodest delight in telling an interviewer: "I don't know how I'm going to explain that to Garner when I get back to Hollywood."

And an influx of Martial Artists to Hong Kong, publicised as hoping to be as "lucky" as Bruce Lee, set his hackles high: "They think they can be lucky, too. Well, I don't believe in pure luck. You have to create your own luck. You have to be aware of the opportunities around you and take advantage of them. Some guys may not believe it, but I spent hours perfecting whatever I did."

But perhaps the most disappointing story of all, if true, is the one about his treatment of a guest at a party who failed to recognise him. Lee pushed his open palm aggressively towards the offending individual and snapped: "Bruce Lee - Movie Star!"

As nobody ever claimed perfection for Lee - at least not in the social graces - it may seem unfair to emphasise such unfortunate moments. But they are necessary in any understanding of the man coping with his success - or failing to cope with it. And there are the other stories. John Saxon of Enter the Dragon insists that Lee did not let his fame impede his relationship with the ordinary people of Hong Kong "... who loved him. They really reacted to him, and he enjoyed them. He enjoyed kibitzing with the cab drivers, with the kids from the age of five or so who recognised and adulated him. It was a pleasure to watch, rather than some people with public positions who don't like to mingle and who say, 'Get them off my back!' or 'I don't want to be bothered!' or 'Get me out of here!' I mean, it really was a problem, but Bruce enjoyed it to the point where it wasn't a problem anymore."

Lee himself had few illusions about the detrimental effects that some of stardom's pressures occasionally had on him. Asked about these not long before his death, he laughed and said: "Let's put it this way: to be honest, I'm not as bad as some others. But I am definitely not a saint."

And in the same interview, he reaffirmed the only philosophy that he could ever really be true to, by saying: "I never believe in the word Star. That's an illusion, man, something the public calls you. When you become successful, when you become famous, it's very very easy to be blinded by all these happenings. Everybody comes up and calls you 'Mr. Lee.' When you have long hair they all say, 'Hey, man, that's in, that's the in thing.' But if you have no name, they all say, 'Look at the disgusting juvenile delinquent!' I mean, too many people are 'Yes, yes, yes to you all the time; so unless you realise what life is all about and that some game is happening, and realise that it is a game, fine and dandy, that's alright.

"But most people tend to be blinded by it, because if things are repeated too many times, you believe them. And that can become a habit."

The rarefied atmosphere of superstardom was certainly fraught with risks for the personality of Bruce Lee.

Shortly before he died, Lee ordered from its British makers, a Rolls Royce Corniche, equipped with a TV set and a radio-phone. It was the kind of bonus of superstardom that most grubby kids on the backstreets of Hong Kong must dream of acquiring: the final symbol of success. Lee explained what he intended to do with the car on delivery: "When the Rolls arrives, I know exactly what I'm going to do. I'm going to motor down to the waterfront and call Roman Polanski and Steve McQueen on the car phone.

"And when they ask where I'm calling from, I'll say from the back seat of my Rolls Royce, overlooking the junks in Hong Kong harbour."

Lee never got to make that telephone call, he died a few days before the car was due to be delivered. But the story shows that the rarefied atmosphere of stardom had certain unusual effects on the character of Bruce Lee. There were risks at his newfound level, risks that he could not use his strength of body to combat.

But they were risks that he acknowledged and accepted - even enjoyed the challenge of facing. For Lee himself had said, some years before the maxim ever looked like applying to him: "Greatness requires the taking of risks. That's why so few ever achieve it."

CHAPTER TEN

THE HIDDEN MAN
On Himself, Life and Truth

"Great Lakes might be boiling around him, yet he would not feel the heat; the Ho and the Han might be frozen up, and he would not feel the cold; thunderbolts may split the mountains and the wind shake the sea, but he will remain unafraid.
Neither death nor life changes him; such abeing he mounts the clouds, rides the sun and moon, and rambles at ease beyond the four seas."

- NIEH CH'UEH

THE HIDDEN MAN
On Himself, Life and Truth

> *"Great Lakes might be boiling around him, yet he would not feel the heat; the Ho and the Han might be frozen up, and he would not feel the cold; thunderbolts may split the mountains and the wind shake the sea, but he will remain unafraid. Neither death nor life changes him; such a being he mounts the clouds, rides the sun and moon, and rambles at ease beyond the four seas."*
>
> *- NIEH CH'UEH*

It is the case with greatness that the personality behind the brilliant veneer is too seldom observed. Or, if it is observed, this is through a visual colander which carefully mitres out any flaw or imperfection, leaving an incomplete portrait.

In Bruce Lee's case, it would be only too easy to present a picture of a man whose private life and personal relationships were as perfect and as flawless as his smooth rise to fame. There have been publications and 'documentary' portraits in plenty, which claim to show the hidden man, set out with the best of intentions to do so, and end by asking us to believe in a demigod who lived a life of little turmoil, miniscule stress, and hardly any personal conflict worth speaking of.

But it would be flying in the face of truth to present such a picture here, it would be betraying our subject to pretend that his was a carefree life, without complications or woeful consequences. Lee was not a perfect man, and he recognised the fact. He was a man of deep and complex nature, whose explorations of himself make for a fascinating, truthful study of a remarkable personality.

His good points, those which are paramount in most portraits, were of course utterly charming. Linda's mother, who initially disliked this robust young Chinese of whom her daughter was so fond, soon found herself captivated by Bruce - as she would surely have been by any young man who could gaze at her so adoringly and say:

"You know, mom, you've got the greatest legs of any woman of your age I've ever seen!"

Friends constantly attest to his brilliance in conversation, to the articulate flow of argument that he would use to electrify any company, no matter how elevated. When he first began to be noticed in America, and attracted the company of established Hollywood stars, it was Lee that everybody listened to at a dinner table containing senators, directors, producers, and movie-idols. His, said one acquired acquaintance, was the only voice that you seemed to hear.

Stirling Silliphant always claimed that Lee was the most exciting person that he had ever met, that his combination of dynamic energy and superb talents made him unforgettable company. Jim Kelly said: "I could listen to him talk all day, all night. He talked about himself a lot. But he had a lot to say. It was like listening to Muhammad Ali talk; same thing..."

Some compliment! But Lee's wit was indeed legendary in his own social circles. It

was said that his memory for jokes and funny stories was so retentive that he could go on telling them for three hours, until the candles were low and the company helpless on the floor. His ability to dramatise was used to its fullest extent in such situations, Peter Chin recalls: "Bruce could be funny about anything like having a pair of trousers made, he could repeat a joke you'd already heard - even a corny one - and make you double up."

And the irrepressible Lee was not too selective about who he turned his wit against. At his University Armed Services Reserve, which he hated, he was once caught chewing gum on parade by a sergeant, who automatically ordered him to "swallow it." Lee, the health and fitness fanatic, would do no such thing. But instead of simply spitting it out when the sergeant's back was turned and forgetting the subject, he spat it down in front of the officer, and by way of explanation, grinned: "It's bad for my health!" The sergeant moved close to Lee, and breathed: "Next time I say swallow, son, you swallow." "And the next time you speak to me like that," replied Lee, "you end up on your back." Miraculously, he escaped disciplinary action that time. The sergeant wandered off with a bemused expression, scratching his head.

Journalists and workmates would also attest to his ability to delight and amuse even a Monday morning movie lot. He could stroll happily into the offices, cracking jokes, waving good morning to everybody, even people he'd never seen before - "Uh, sorry, case

of mistaken identity. But good morning all the same." He'd stop to massage a secretary's neck because she complains of an ache, and begin to sing. When he'd finished his song, Lee would beam at the company: "If there's one thing I'm certain of, it is the fact that I can't sing. I tell people I have a rich voice - because it's well off!" And follow that by cheerfully admitting: "I write my own scripts in Chinese first. Then somebody has to polish it up a bit, because my Chinese is getting a bit rusty!"

One time on the set of *Enter the Dragon*, a Chinese journalist wanted to interview Jim Kelly, but he couldn't speak English. Lee offered to act as interpreter, and was told: "Okay, then, Bruce - ask Jim what he thinks of Bruce Lee." Deadpan, Lee did just that. And equally straight-faced, Kelly replied: "Hey, Bruce, you tell him that Bruce Lee talks a lot of bullshit. But he can back up his bullshit." Then the three exploded in laughter. Of course, women younger than Linda's mother could also expect to be charmed off their feet. He had a set of cards printed, which he would hand to girls that he'd just met for the first time. On them was printed: If you'd like to go to bed with me, smile now! It seems odd, then, that this same ebullient Bruce Lee could turn to his wife at times with doubt written large across his face and say: "I am difficult to live with, aren't I?"

Or that he could, in private notes and jottings, accuse himself of what he called

"self-image actualisation." What he meant was that the overwhelming urge for expansion and growth, and the achievement of recognition and fame, had led him to ignore his true self in favour of some false image of Bruce Lee. He shamefully noted that he once had got a kick out of this image, and resolved: "The greatest help is self-help; there is no other help but self-help - doing one's best, dedicating oneself wholeheartedly to a given task, which happens to have no end but is an on-going process. I have done a lot during these years of my process. Well, in my process, I have changed from self-image actualisation to self-actualisation, from blindly following propaganda, organised truths, etc., to search internally for the cause of my ignorance."

Lee seemed to use the same power of ambition and force of character that got him stardom and riches, to achieve the very different end of personal peace and well-being. It is almost as if when he said: "I'll never say I'm number one. But I'll never admit to being number two."

He was referring, not only to the Martial Arts or to the cinema, but also to spiritual affairs, placidity, honesty, and goodness. He would speak of a force which he felt within himself, which was almost untapped, and which defied description, but was "something like a strong emotion mixed with faith." And he would go on to say: "All in all, the goal of my planning and doing is to find the true meaning in life - peace of mind."

Lee realised, and said so, that wealth, fame, possessions, etc., did not necessarily and automatically bring about this "peace of mind," and indeed might obstruct his attaining it. But he determined to devote himself to what he called "real accomplishment" rather than "neurotic combat," and consequently utilize the teachings of Taoism and Zen.

He also denied that he was too eager for success, saying that his desire to do more

and more sprung rather from a knowledge of his own capacities than a rapacious, over-eager longing for recognition. And as he rightly pointed out: "Success comes to those who are success-conscious. If you don't aim at an object how the heck on earth do you think you can get it?"

So in fact, all of the Ali-type superlatives about his own future, all of the "I'll be the biggest" and the "I'm not going to be an actor, I'm going to be a star" type of statement sprang from a fundamental understanding of his own future and capabilities, rather than from self-aggrandisement and wishful thinking. Lee had to be the biggest, because he knew he was the best.

In saying to Steve McQueen, "Know yourself," he was actually saying, as McQueen fully understood: "Not only in the Martial Arts must you understand your failures and your potential, but also in life."

McQueen says: "The good head that he acquired was through his knowing himself. He and I used to have great long discussions about that. No matter what you do in life, if you don't know yourself, you're never going to be able to appreciate anything in life. That, I think, is today's mark of a good human being - to know yourself."

By the same token, when Lee would ask people to feel and admire his muscles, when he demonstrated in what might seem to be a conceited manner his great physique, he was simply pointing to an achievement of which he had every right to be proud, as a painter exhibits his work. Andre Morgan of Golden Harvest films remembers this perfectionism: "He could be very annoying, he wanted things to be just right. For example, he spent a whole morning doing one fight sequence, something like a dozen takes. We viewed the rushes. The third, fourth, and fifth takes were all good and yet he had gone on and done the sixth, seventh, eighth and so on, because at the time he didn't feel comfortable about them."

In rehearsing with nunchaku sticks, he would go on until hardly able to move his arms and shoulders for the bruises. As Lee himself admitted: "I don't want to do anything halfway. It has to be perfect."

And as Danny Inosanto said of his old master and colleague: "He was of a calibre far beyond other Martial Artists. He's the Edison, Einstein, and Leonardo da Vinci of the Martial Arts. Bruce reminded us of Jonathan Livingston Seagull because he was always striving to be better and better. If he had any shortcomings, he was such a perfectionist he couldn't stand anything that didn't come up to his standards."

But behind it all, there was some doubt in the mind of the perfectionist. Not as to how much he was capable of, of that he had no doubt: "There is no limit, no end in sight, to how far I can ascend in my knowledge of acting and the Martial Arts."

Rather, there was a nagging feeling that the giant steps he was taking into uncharted areas of human achievement might be fraught with more danger than anybody had (or could have) predicted, and which made him confide, querulously, to Linda: "I don't know for how long I can keep this up."

When such dark thoughts emerged from the recesses of his troubled mind, it was to

Linda that Lee would turn. It would be absurd to pretend that he was constantly faithful to her, that other women never entered his life. They did. Stirling Silliphant recalls times when Lee would take him out to lunch with two beautiful girls. Silliphant usually had to leave after lunch, despite Lee's protestations, but would be amply regaled later by Lee's tales of "what a wonderful time you missed there, man." And the story of Lee's relationship with the beautiful Betty Ting Pei, in whose flat he died, although shrouded with mystery is obviously the story of a love-affair.

But it is equally obvious that his relationship with Linda was the anchor of his life. Linda herself recalls him telling her that he considered incidental affairs with other women to be irrelevant, of absolutely no significance when set against the importance of his love for Linda and the children. They discussed a couple who had split up, some friends of theirs, where the husband had found another woman and the wife had simply hung around, inviting sympathy and making a social virtue out of being forlorn, for years. Linda made it clear that her response would be completely different - she would just leave him for good.

Lee, she knew, could not stand such a parting. He many times avowed that the most vital things in life to him, the major stabilising influence, were Linda and the children. He also knew that no couple, no union, had ever been perfect or was ever likely to be, and he would say: "I'm not in this world to live up to your expectations, and you're not in this world to live up to mine."

Such was his closeness to Linda, then, that it is in his letters to her that many of the confidences and secret hopes that tell much about Lee was expressed. Probably the most interesting bunch of mail,, written at an equally interesting period in his career, during the filming of *The Big Boss* in Pak Chong, Thailand.

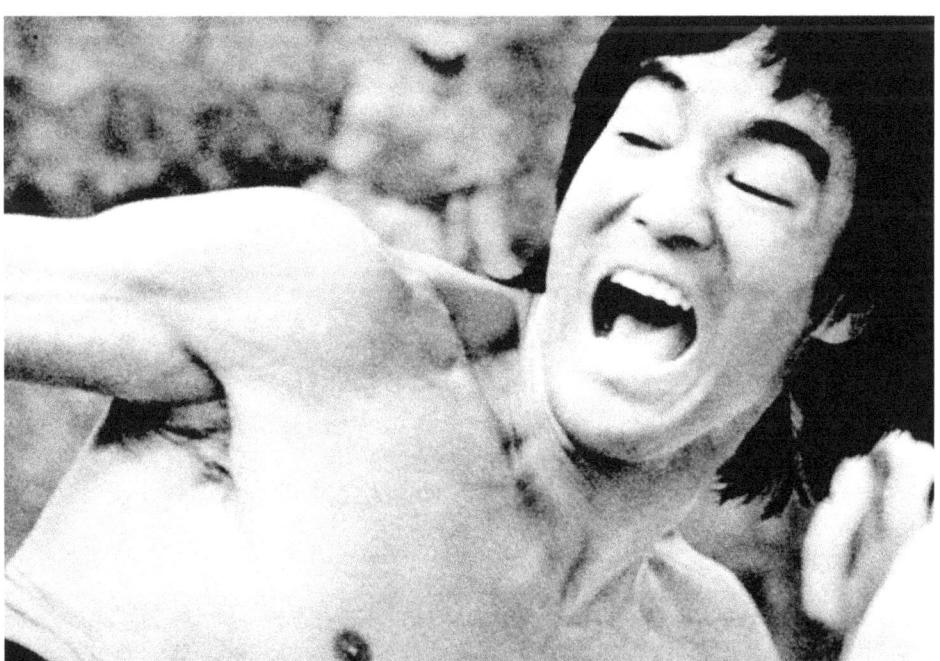

He had arrived back in the East already halfway a star, trailing the comparatively muted clouds of glory from his television appearances behind him. So the press had taken an interest - and their interest had been amplified on discovery that this young man was as garrulous as he was handsome. Lee made it clear that his films were to be about Chinese subjects, and he was proud of it. "People are just plain stupid to let themselves be oppressed."

He went on to the subject of American affluence: "Sure, money is important in providing for my family and giving us what we want. But it isn't everything."

Bruce also gave a quick treatise on the art of spending money correctly: "I don't think putting smoke into your body is quite the thing to do. As for alcohol, I think it tastes awful. Don't know why anyone should want to drink the stuff. As for gambling, I don't believe in getting something for nothing. But I do buy lots of clothes, although I seldom have the chance to show them off since I go out infrequently."

He rounded it off on a comparison between social life in Hong Kong and in America: "When I first arrived, I did *The Green Hornet* television series back in '65, and as I looked around, man, I saw a lot of human beings. And as I looked at myself, I saw I was the only robot there.

"I was not being myself. I was trying to accumulate external security - external technique - the way to move my arm and so on, but I was never asking what Bruce Lee would have done.

"When I look around, I always learn something, and that is to be yourself. And to express yourself, to have faith in yourself. Do not go out and look for a successful personality and duplicate him. That seems to me to be the prevalent thing happening in Hong Kong. They always copy mannerism, they never start from the very root of their being: that is, how can I be me?"

With such homilies out of the way, and after a quick joke about his wife ("She's picking up Chinese cooking very well"), and Brandon his son ("The only blond-haired, blue-eyed Chinaman in California"), Lee was whisked off to the wilderness north of Bangkok. And, frank as he might have been to the press, he was doubly so to Linda in the series of letters that ensued.

Lee did not like Pak Chong, and had his doubts about its importance to his career. Events there seemed to be weighed against him. The mosquitoes and cockroaches were plentiful, and he apologised for being late in writing to Linda, explaining that he had cut his hand when a glass he was washing up broke, and he needed ten stitches, rendering it difficult for him to take a bath, let alone write a letter!

He then revealed that Golden Harvest - the company belonging to Raymond Chow that Lee was working for - would only pay for Linda's airfare to the East if Lee did a short film on Jeet Kune Do for them. He added that it seemed unlikely that they would press the point, however, as "I'm the superstar in Hong Kong," and even the Shaw Bros, were trying to get him. Lee complained bitterly that there was a shortage of meat in Pak Chong, expressing relief that he'd brought along his vitamin pills, and disgust at having to eat canned meat for lunch.

"It's been fifteen days since my arrival in Pak Chong," he wrote, "and it seems already like a year."

On top of local discomforts, Lee found the director, Lo Wei, to be unbearable, and what was worse: untalented; he thought the studio set-up amateurish; and he lost his voice after too much screaming in fight scenes. He looked forward to moving on to Bangkok.

It was in Bangkok that Lee first got wind of the extraordinary turbulence that had been started in the civilised world by the first showing of Paramount's *Longstreet*. Where previously The Green Hornet and his Martial Arts reputation might have made him "a superstar in Hong Kong," now he was on the verge of becoming a worldwide superstar. "Like the song says," he wrote to Linda, "We've only just begun."

Lee's luck in Thailand, however, despite such promising days ahead, did not change. Linda was told that he had sprained his ankle after a high jump, and caught flu on his way to see a doctor in Bangkok. Despite such depressing circumstances, though, Lee remembered enough to wish Linda a happy anniversary, and inform her that he had been able to get her a present - to be revealed in more comfortable surroundings. And as Linda, in the States, was having to act as a kind of agent in Lee's dealings with Paramount, he informed her of his plans to work for them after a month's rest at the end of filming The Big Boss. And there is a kind of elation in Lee's writing the lines: "Its about time to raise my worth - my future in acting has now begun. I'm sure the one I'm doing now *(The Big Boss)* will be a big success - again, time will tell. Though the place I'm in is rather hell, I'm in the profession where I belong and love to do."

And in a momentary lapse from Lee's normally supreme confidence, we see the young Chinese who still could not quite believe that Hollywood, the "magic kingdom," wanted him at last, who was still obliged to prepare his spirit for another disappointment: "If Paramount really likes me," he wrote to Linda, "and if I really did such a good job, I feel I should advance to at least two grand ($2000) per episode. Who knows what the future holds? There comes a time when you have to advance or retreat; this time I can always retreat to my Hong Kong deal."

Lee's relationship with his wife is, of course, a useful guide to more than just the workings of his inner mind during great moments in his career. It also shows us a side of the man too frequently neglected by his portrayers: the sentimentalist, who loved the idea of family, wife and children as much as the actuality; and who was capable of expressing that love in poetic terms. Linda remembers Lee describing his feelings in the following words: "Love is like a friendship caught on fire. In the beginning a flame, very pretty, often hot and fierce but still only light and flickering. As love grows older, our hearts mature and our love becomes as coals, deep-burning and unquenchable."

Fred Weintraub of Warner Bros, remembers the dependence of Lee on Linda, and has said that she was the only person that he seemed able to trust, and he deposited that trust in her with an almost childlike faith - "She was wife, mother, mistress, lover, everything." If Lee had argued with somebody and later repented of his temper, he would get Linda to 'phone them and apologise, or rather (as Lee disliked apologising for anything) to tell them that no bad blood remained, that the quarrel was forgotten. Linda agrees that she was able to complement his character, filling in with patience and calm the intolerance and unrest that Lee often displayed.

"Our marriage," she has said, "was not like the mathematical equation where one plus one equals two, but rather that two halves fitted snugly together to represent a whole."

Among his friends and those who knew him well, Lee's generosity was a by-word. It was an unusual kind of generosity for Hollywood, or indeed any area of the movie world, manifesting not in flash parties or expensive clothes for expensive women, but in more intimate, thoughtful ways. It was essentially a generosity of the soul, as if the same despising of cant and humbug that made him once exclaim: "What I detest most is dishonest people who talk more than they are capable of doing. I also find people obnoxious who use false humility as a means to cover their inadequacy."

It also made him feel obliged to follow the bigness of his success with a bigness of heart. Herb Jackson recalls: "Bruce was a true friend, honest almost to a fault. The few times he used criticism, it was biting because his words had the ring of truth in them. He was also the most generous person I have ever known. Once in Hong Kong, I was admiring a beautiful suede suit of his. He showed me the quality of the material, the silk lining, and explained how it was specially made - one of a kind. "He said: 'See how you look in it, Herb,' and then he said: 'It's yours.' Just like that."

Dan Inosanto tells a story which indicates a different kind of generosity, the desire to understand his friends and assist them, not only in material ways: "I was kind of shy,

THE WISDOM OF BRUCE LEE

bashful, and I think he (Bruce) helped my personality in that respect, that he taught me to be confident and more outgoing. "He asked me: 'Why are you bashful? Have you ever thought of that, Dan?' And I said, 'Well, I guess I'm scared of people.' He asked, 'Why are you scared of people?' and I answered, 'Well, I'm scared of making mistakes.' He came back with, 'What could happen to you if you did make a mistake in public?' and I then listed the things that could happen - the worst things that could possibly happen. I guess he used the Socratic method because he would never answer for me. He would always let me answer."

Wally Jay, who runs a Martial Arts club in California, discovered the practical side of Lee's open-heartedness. Jay had met Lee in Seattle in the early days, when Jay taught boxing and Lee was an astonishingly gifted student of the Martial Arts. The two men became friends through mutual admiration and interests, and it was friendship that Lee never forgot. He would appear at benefit performances for Jay's club even when his time was valued at thousands of dollars the hour, and accept no payment, explaining to accountants: "It is a benefit for Island Judo Club, and I only want my airfare paid."

His old school in Hong Kong, the Saint Francis Xavier academy, was also to be thankful for Lee's long memory and generous spirit. In 1973, Brother Gregory the college principal was surprised to receive a telephone call from Lee. In conversation, Brother Gregory slipped in a mention of the prize-giving ceremonies due soon, and would it be possible? Lee laughingly agreed: "Of course, I'd be delighted."

Brother Gregory adds: "I think that is what impressed the boys more than anything else; the fact that famous as he was, he came back as a sign of gratitude to his old teachers. He was a real friend - a hero."

Lee's pride in his body is, of course, well-known. It was his major asset, and he recognised it as such, nurturing and caring for it. Fred Weintraub called him "the most protective guy for his own physical well-being I ever met." Partly, this obsession with fitness was due to his detestation of being incapacitated by illness. One reason for this was the responsibility that he deeply felt towards his wife and children's upkeep. Once he had been offered $10,000 to teach a group of European industrialists the Martial Arts for two weeks. Unfortunately, Lee had recently injured his back in training and had to turn the offer down. It worried him: "This was the first time in my life I was really scared," he admitted. "If I hadn't had a family it wouldn't have been so bad. But having a wife and two children made me realise that having bread is important."

Even more gnawing, though, was the forced routine of being confined to bed. Lee detested such inactivity: "I never wanted a job in an office or any job that I had to work eight hours a day at - day in and day out. I don't think I could have stood it."

As it was, Lee often found the pressures of a "free-curriculum" superstar's life difficult and tiresome. He often spoke of the problems of a life in the public eye and constantly stressed to friends the difficulties of relaxation in such circumstances.
"The biggest detriment to relaxation," he told Linda, "is to say: I will relax."
When Lee first collapsed in Hong Kong, and was rushed to the hospital, he woke up to find his wife smiling down at him. He told her that he had been very close to death over the last few hours, and that he was prepared to struggle with all his being: "I'm going to fight it - I'm going to make it - I'm not going to give up."

It was not that Lee feared death particularly. One of his favourite songs was titled

And when I Die, and contains the line: "If it's peace you find dying, well then let the time be near." He had often commented, ruefully, on hearing that line: "Maybe that's the only place where I'll find peace."

He had never been afraid to discuss the subject with friends, frequently remarking: "If I should die tomorrow, I will have no regrets. I did what I wanted to do. You can't expect much more from life."

No, Lee was not afraid of death. But to go with so much left undone! To die with so full and important a life beckoning him ahead! For a man who had waited, by virtue of his colour and creed, so inordinately long for recognition, the possibility of early death must have been particularly cruel.

Lee once told his biographer, Alex Ben Block, when the latter asked him if he believed in God: "To be perfectly frank, I really do not." Linda Lee later qualified this remark of her husband's, saying that he believed God to be within the soul of man, to be the composer of man's "inner theme." Lee had seen his end in similar terms: "The soul of man is an embryo in the body of man. The day of death is the day of awakening. The spirit lives on."

And: "To learn to die is to be liberated from it. When tomorrow comes, you must learn to die and be liberated from it."

There are some of Bruce Lee's sayings, some of the phrases that he chose to use, wisdoms he liked to express, and actions that demonstrate a part of his character, that are simply unclassifiable. Thus far in this book, the authors have attempted to order his opinions and ideas into various pigeonholes - the Martial Arts, films, Hollywood, etc. But the human mind does not operate in so orderly a fashion, and Lee's mind was no exception.

What follows, then, is an amalgam of the unclassifiable. It is a collection of Lee's thoughts and sayings on the broader themes of life and truth.

In his spare time, it was a hobby of Lee's to translate Chinese poetry into English. His choice of poetry was as capable as was his actual translation.

These are two of them:

> "Rain Black clouds,
> Fallen blossoms and pale moon,
> The hurried flight of birds,
> The arrival of lonely autumn,
> The time for us to part.
> Much has been said, yet
> We have not come to the end of our feeling.
> I leave you this poem
> Read it when the silence of the world possesses you,
> Or when you're fretted with disquiet,
> Long must be this parting, and
> Remember,
> That all my thoughts have always been of you."

The following poem, by the Chinese master Tzu Yeh, was also translated by Lee:

> Young man.
> Seize every minute
> Of your time
> The days fly by;
> Ere long you too
> Will grow old.
> If you believe me not
> See here, in the courtyard,
> How the frost
> Glitters white and cold and cruel
> On the grass
> That once was green.
> Do you not see
> That you and I
> Are as the branches
> Of one tree
> With your rejoicing
> Comes my laughter;
> With your sadness
> Start my tears.
> Love,
> Could life be otherwise,
> With you and me?

As well as expressing himself through verse, Lee would frequently use the time-honoured Chinese style of poetic aphorism; the kind of brief truism that is known in the West. Lee would jot these brief lines down, as a way of disciplining his thoughts.

There follows just a few of them:

"To change with change is the changeless state."

"Not being tense but ready. Not thinking but not dreaming. Not being set but flexible. Liberation from the uneasy sense of confinement. It is being wholly and quietly alive, aware and alert, ready for whatever may come."

"Man, because he is a creative individual, is far more important than any style or system."

"Life is a constant process of relating."

"Liberating truth is a reality only in so far as it is experienced and lived by the individual himself; it is a truth that transcends styles or disciplines."

"A person cannot forget someone who is good to them."

"Knowing is not enough; we must apply. Willing is not enough; we must do."

"A good teacher protects his pupils from his own influence."

"A fat belly cannot believe that such a thing as hunger exists."

"Real living is living for others."

"Becoming a human being is an act."

"True refinement seeks simplicity."

"It's the will that makes men - success takes perseverance."

"Empty heads have long tongues."

"If every man would help his neighbour, no man would be without help."

"Yesterdays dreams are often tomorrow's realities."

"If you want to do your duty properly, you should do just a little more than that."

"Pessimism blunts the tools you need to succeed."

"Optimism is a faith that leads to success."

"A goal is not always meant to be reached, it often serves simply as something to aim at."

"One great cause of failure is lack of concentration."

"Showing off is the fool's idea of glory."

"If you don't want to slip up tomorrow, speak the truth today."

"Knowledge will give you power, but character will give you respect."

"Self-education makes great men."

"If you think a thing is impossible, you'll make it impossible."

"If you love life, don't waste time, for time is what life is made up of."

Even in the most mundane aspects of day-to-day life and communication, Lee was capable of stirring insight. After his friend, Taky Kimura, had split up with his wife and was exceptionally depressed, Lee sent him the following letter: "In life, there are the pluses and the minuses, and it is time for you to concentrate on the pluses. It might be difficult, but fortunately for us human beings, we have self-will. Well, it is time to employ it.

"Life is an ever-flowing process and somewhere on the path some unpleasant things will pop up-it might leave a scar, but then life is flowing on and like running water, when it stops, it grows stale. Go bravely on, my friend, because each experience teaches us a lesson, and remember, if there is anything at all I can help with, let me know.

"Keep blasting - life is such that sometimes it is nice, and sometimes it is not."

Finally, Lee would quote these lines from the great Chinese poet Lao-Tzu to illustrate his philosophy of the Martial Arts. It is difficult to read them now without realising just how much they epitomise his entire outlook on life:

> *"Alive, a man is supple, soft;*
> *In death, unbending, rigorous.*
> *All creatures, grass and trees, alive*
> *Are plastic but are pliant too*
> *And dead, are friable and dry.*
> *Unbending rigor is the mate of death,*
> *And yielding softness, company of life;*
> *Unbending soldiers get no victories;*
> *The stiffest tree is readiest for the axe.*
> *The strong and mighty topple from their*
> *place; The soft and yielding rise above them all."*

After his death, it became easy to misinterpret these ideas and statements, to see Bruce Lee as having been the possessor of, if not exactly a death wish, at least a morbid trait which encouraged him to anticipate death. Lee himself would have mocked at such theories. Rather than worrying himself into an early grave, he was too fast and alive to live, too full of his existence and love of what he did, he gave too much to life. Phil Ochs, the American folk-singer, mourned him with these words: "There were rumours in Hollywood of cocaine. Maybe he was killed by some crazy person or some rival business faction. Maybe he lived more intensely than any human being can live. Or maybe he died for the same reason James Dean died. They had taken too much of the fire, and the gods were jealous."

But with her knowledge of the man behind the fire, the inner man who stole her heart a decade before he stole the world's, with his perfect grace and deific style, Linda told radio Hong Kong: "I know that a lot of things are being said now that make it seem that he wasn't always as beautiful as I think he was. But so much of what is said you must not believe, because it's rumour and it's absolutely untrue. He was just a human being, he wasn't perfect, but he was a very, very beautiful person inside. He was always very good to me. I could not have a complaint in the world - I could not wish for a better husband, ever."

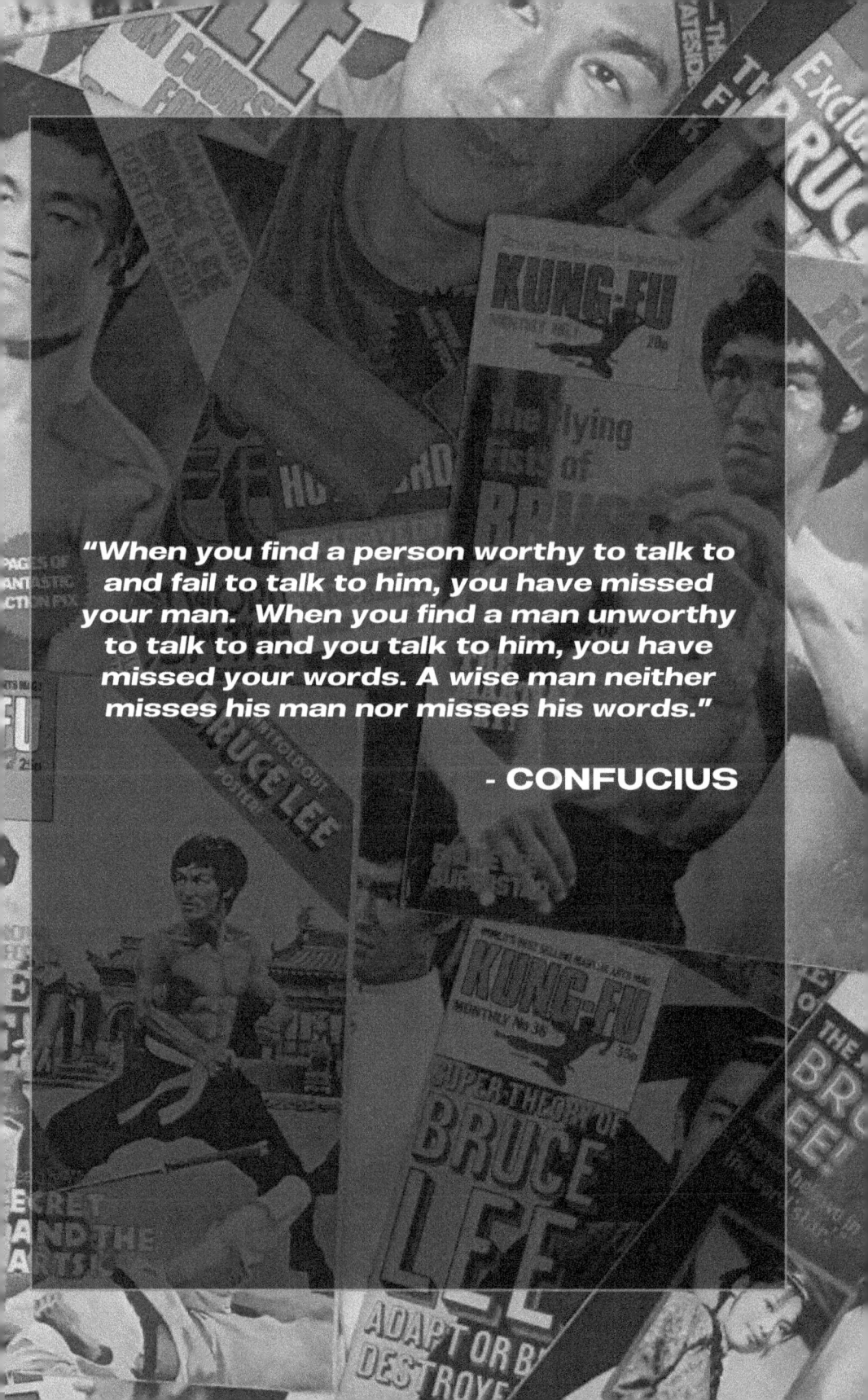

"When you find a person worthy to talk to and fail to talk to him, you have missed your man. When you find a man unworthy to talk to and you talk to him, you have missed your words. A wise man neither misses his man nor misses his words."

- CONFUCIUS

THE WISDOM OF BRUCE LEE

THE ARCHIVE SERIES
THE WISDOM OF BRUCE LEE

BIBLIOGRAPHY AND PHOTO CREDIT

BIBLIOGRAPHY

The Beginners Guide to Kung-Fu by Felix Dennis & Paul Simmons (Wildwood House/Bunch Books 1974); *The Book of Kung-Fu* by Various Authors (Bunch Books 1974); *Bruce Lee King of Kung-Fu* by Felix Dennis & Don Atyeo (Wildwood House/Bunch Books 1974); *Secret Fighting Arts Of The World* by John F. Gilby (Charles E. Tuttle 1963); *The Legend of Bruce Lee* by Alex Ben Block (Dell 1974); *The Wisdom of Kung-Fu* by Michael Minick (Morrow 1974); *Kung-Fu Cinema of Vengeance* by V. Glaessner (Lorrimer 1974); *Bruce Lee: The Man Only I Knew* by Linda Lee (Warner Paperback Library 1975); *170 Chinese Poems* Translated by Arthur Waley (Jonathan Cape 1967); *Bruce Lee 1940-1973* by Various Authors (Ohara Publications 1974); *The Tao of Jeet Kune Do* by Bruce Lee (Ohara Publications 1975); *Chinese Leg Manoeuvres* by Lee Ying-Arng (Unicorn Press 1962).

The books above represent only a fraction of the sources from which the authors prepared the groundwork for this book. Especially recommended are *The Tao of Jeet Kune Do* by Bruce Lee, *Bruce Lee The Man Only I Knew* by Lee's wife, Linda and *The Legend of Bruce Lee* by Alex Block. It would be impossible to list all the magazines from which the authors have taken notes, quotes, and information, especially those published in Hong Kong. We would mention especially only *Black Belt* from the U.S.A., probably the finest Martial Arts magazine in the world today and *Kung-Fu Monthly* in Great Britain. We would also like to thank the anonymous members of Bruce Lee's family who gave us so much of their time and patience.

Since the original publication of this book, the editors would also like to recommend *The Warrior Within* by John Little, *The Bruce Lee Library Series* by Tuttle Books and *Dynamic Becoming* by James Bishop.

PHOTO CREDITS

The photographs in the original publications of *The Wisdom of Bruce Lee* were published with permission from H. Bunch & Associates Ltd. London, Peter Bennett, Golden Harvest Films Hong Kong, Brother Gregory of Saint Francis Xavier College, Warner Bros Films/Concord Films, UPI, Chester Maydole and Perry Neville and are reproduced here.

ALSO BY THE AUTHOR

THE K.F.M. BRUCE LEE SOCIETY

"BEAUTIFULLY CAPTURES THE HEART, SOUL, AND SPIRIT OF THE UNITED KINGDOM'S FLEDGLING BRUCE LEE FANBASE. UNDENIABLY COLLECTIBLE."

- BRUCE LEE REVIEW

"NOT JUST A COMPILATION OF NOSTALGIC NEWSLETTERS, BUT A BRITISH HISTORY GUIDE TO A PERIOD TIME WHEN WESTERN PEOPLE DISCOVERED THE UNIQUE TALENTS OF THE UNDISPUTED KING OF KUNG FU - BRUCE LEE."

- ANDREW J. STATON, BRITISH JUN FAN JOURNAL

"THANK YOU VERY MUCH FOR YOUR TIME AND EFFORT TO HONOUR PAM FOR HER GREAT WORK AND DEDICATION. I, TOGETHER WITH THE BRUCE LEE FANS WHO KNEW PAM SALUTE YOU!"

- ROBERT LEE

THE **KUNG-FU MONTHLY** BRUCE LEE SECRET SOCIETY BEGAN IN SEPTEMBER 1976, RUNNING FOR 30 ISSUES BEFORE IT'S FINAL ISSUE IN SEPTEMBER 1983. RUN BY THE FORMIDABLE PAM HADDEN, THE BRUCE LEE SECRET SOCIETY FUNCTIONED AS THE SOURCE OF INFORMATION FOR BRUCE LEE FANS IN THE UK AND LATER, THE REST OF THE WORLD. FOR THE FIRST TIME EVER, ALL 30 ISSUES HAVE BEEN PAINSTAKINGLY RE-EDITED AND RE-PRINTED IN THIS BOOK, ALONG WITH UPDATED NOTES AND RETROSPECTIVE STORIES BY THE PEOPLE MOST RESPONSIBLE FOR KEEPING BRUCE LEE'S MEMORY ALIVE - THE FANS.

AVAILABLE FROM **WWW.KUNGFUMONTHLY.UK & AMAZON**

THE WORLD FAMOUS
MARKETPLACE

DON'T FORGET TO VISIT OUR WEBSITE FOR OTHER FANTASTIC ITEMS INCLUDING CLOTHING AND LIMITED EDITION SETS!

◀ BRUCE LEE
KING OF KUNG FU

Written by Felix Dennis & Don Atyeo, Bruce Lee King of Kung Fu is the original and still one of the greatest books on Bruce Lee ever written. Packed with photos and essential information from the immediate year after Lee's tragic death, Bruce Lee King of Kung Fu provides the best of rock-solid backgrounds to the story of the man we all know and love.
170 PAGES

BUY ONLINE NOW!

amazon
WHSmith
Waterstones

OR VISIT OUR WEBSITE AT
WWW.KUNGFUMONTHLY.UK

KUNG-FU MONTHLY ▶
THE POSTER MAGAZINES

Volume One - No. 1 to 25, trade dummy plus an in-depth article on The History of Kung-Fu Monthly 1973 to 1979.
Volume Two - No. 26 to 55 plus interviews with former KFM staff.
Volume Three - No. 56 to 79, double-poster special edition issue plus an in-depth article on The History of Kung-Fu Monthly 1980 to 1984.
540-670 PAGES

THE BOOK OF ▶
KUNG FU

The Book of Kung Fu was to be Kung-Fu Monthly's special annual issue, but was only published in 1974. Over one-hundred pages, many of them in colour, with a durable soft cover and scores of photographs, illustrations and articles. Don't miss this book! Bruce Lee, Angela Mao, David Carradine. Kung Fu Quiz, Comic Book and more - an incredible publication!
144 PAGES

THE SECRET ART OF ▶
BRUCE LEE

In 1976, the world took its first look at the now legendary Chester Maydole photographs. Arranged where possible, in 'fast-frame' action sequences, The Secret Art of Bruce Lee shows the founder of Jeet Kune Do, assisted by his friend and student Dan Inosanto, demonstrating the early development state of his art Jeet Kune Do during early days in Los Angeles.
110 PAGES

THE LOST KFM BOOK
FIRST TIME EVER IN THE UK!

◀ THE WISDOM OF BRUCE LEE

The Wisdom of Bruce Lee was to be one of the first books in the world to look at Bruce Lee's philosophy on life and martial arts. Mysteriously never released in the UK, The Wisdom of Bruce Lee is finally available to UK Bruce Lee fans after a wait of over forty years.
The full-length version includes a new introduction and interview with author Roger Hutchinson by Jun Fan Journal writer Andrew Staton, while the shorter abridged version is formatted in the style of the original Kung-Fu Monthly books.
70 PAGES / 170 PAGES

◀ THE UNBEATABLE BRUCE LEE

The Unbeatable Bruce Lee presents readers with a fighter's view of Bruce Lee the man and Bruce Lee the martial arts master. Beneath the sheer weight of known facts and figures that surround the tragically short life of Hong Kong's number one son, lies a strata of truth that only now is beginning to be picked.
112 PAGES

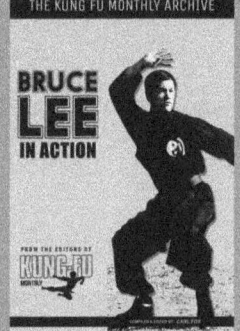

◀ BRUCE LEE IN ACTION

With Bruce Lee in Action, the Editors of Kung-Fu Monthly had compiled another fine addition to their library of Bruce Lee publications. Lavishly illustrated throughout with many previously unseen photographs at the time, this informative book investigates clearly and concisely, the birth and subsequent development of Lee's fighting style Jeet Kune Do, both on and off the screen.
106 PAGES

THE POWER OF ▶ BRUCE LEE

Bruce Lee was possibly the greatest exponent of the martial arts ever produced. The fact that he was a movie star often clouds his enormous contribution to the field. The Power of Bruce Lee explores many of his revolutionary methods of attack and defence, especially those relating to Jeet Kune Do, Lee's name for his own fighting system
110 PAGES

WHO KILLED ▶ BRUCE LEE?

Who Killed Bruce Lee? is a study of the pressures and the forces that, on the one hand were to elevate him to the highest plains of stardom and on the other, were to so tragically strike him down before his final fulfilment.
Who Killed Bruce Lee? was one of the first books to delve deep into the newspaper stories of Lee's early death.
108 PAGES

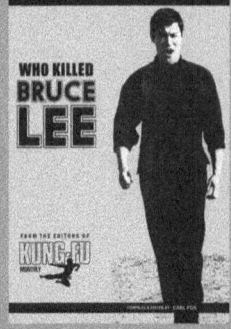

◀ THE GAME OF DEATH

This book combines two Kung-Fu Monthly special edition magazines released prior to Golden Harvest's 1978 film. Researched exclusively in Hong Kong, Kung-Fu Monthly reports on Lee's plot for Game of Death, the cast he intended to appear in the film, the scenes already filmed and Lee's hopes and expectations for the success of the project.Incredibly accurate for the time, this publication represents an important part of Bruce Lee fandom in the UK.
XXX PAGES

FIND OUT MORE INFORMATION AT

THE MAGAZINES

WWW.KUNGFUMONTHLY.UK

◀ THE BEGINNER'S GUIDE TO KUNG FU

Originally released in 1974, The Beginner's Guide to Kung Fu was the first martial arts book aimed primarily at the Kung Fu Craze generation. The graphic, easy to understand illustrations by Paul Simmons and the carefully conceived step by step instructions made this the perfect book for beginners who wished to take up Kung Fu.
XXX PAGES

▲
THE BRUCE LEE SCRAPBOOK

In 1974, Kung-Fu Monthly issued a Bruce Lee scrapbook in the form of a large A3 magazine, followed by a smaller A4 sized book in 1979.
As part of the KFM Archive Series, both scrapbooks have been combined in a new chronological layout with brand new captions, location information and dates by Carl Fox and Jun Fan Journal writer Andrew Staton.
150 PAGES

THE KFM BRUCE LEE SOCIETY ▶

Long before the internet communities we know today, The Bruce Lee Society was the source of information in the United Kingdom for all things Bruce Lee.Now the history of the Bruce Lee Society is finally told in The Bruce Lee Society: A Retrospective Look at Bruce Lee Mania and the Kung Fu Craze of the 1970s. For the first time ever, all thirty issues of The Bruce Lee Society newsletters have been painstakingly re-edited and re-printed in this book, along with updated notes and retrospective stories by the people most responsible for keeping Bruce Lee's memory alive - the fans.
544 PAGES

BRUCE LEE

He was a man of startling contradictions. As a student he excelled in the philosophy and practice of all the ancient fighting arts. As an accomplished Martial Artist his unorthodox methods soon revolutionised Karate and Kung Fu. His creation of Jeet Kune Do, a wholly new style of fighting, firmly established him as a master.

This book is an analysis and an appreciation of the man who truly became a legend in his own time - a warrior whose every thought, word, and action was aimed toward a more perfect combination of philosophy and the art of fighting.

Here is all that is known of the innermost secrets of the incomparable combatant, Bruce Lee, a man who dared to transcend the ancient disciplines and shape them into his own image.

The Wisdom of Bruce Lee was one of the first books to heavily feature Bruce Lee's philosophy and outlook on life and the Martial Arts.

Released in 1976 and written by Roger Hutchinson and Felix Dennis, *The Wisdom of Bruce Lee* was advertised over five pages and two issues of the famous UK poster magazine *Kung-Fu Monthly*. Despite this strong marketing strategy, *The Wisdom of Bruce Lee* was never published in its native United Kingdom. Published in the Netherlands, Germany and Italy, in their respective languages with many colour and black and white photographs, the only English language version appeared in the United States of America with only a handful of black and white photographs.

Pit Wheel Press, as part of their *Kung-Fu Monthly* Archive Series, proudly presents **The Wisdom of Bruce Lee** for the first time in the UK, combining the English text from the USA edition and the photographs from the European editions.

Also exclusively included is a history of the book, *The Wisdom of Bruce Lee: The Enigma of the Lost KFM Book* by Bruce Lee historian Andrew Staton and an interview with the original author Roger Hutchinson.

Special Thanks must go to John Overall for his assistance in sourcing the Dutch language version of *The Wisdom of Bruce Lee* as photographic source material for this edition of the book.

www.ingramcontent.com/pod-product-compliance
Lightning Source LLC
Chambersburg PA
CBHW041154110526
44590CB00027B/4228